Releasing the Inner Magician

VOLUME ONE

DEBORAH L. SANDELLA PH.D., R.N.

Ways to Find a Peaceful and Happy Life

The Inner Magician Series
Denver, Colorado

Grateful acknowledgement is made for permission to reproduce the following material: "Connections" by Nancy Wood, © Nancy Wood from Dancing Moons, Bantam Doubleday Dell, New York 1995. All rights reserved. "Control or Surrender: Altering Approaches to Problem Solving," in The 1989 Annual Developing Human Resources, edited by J. William Pfeiffer, created by Jim Ballard, © University Associates 1989. Reprinted by permission of Jossey-Bass Inc., a subsidiary of John Wiley & Sons, Inc.

Published by
The Inner Magician Series
5082 East Hampden, #244
Denver, Colorado 80222

www.innermagician.com

The author of this book does not dispense medical advice or prescribe the use of any technique as a form of treatment for physical or medical problems without the advice of a physician, either directly or indirectly. The intent of the author is only to offer information of a general nature to help you in your quest for emotional and spiritual well-being. The meditations in this book are tools for self-discovery and are not intended for use by survivors of childhood abuse/trauma. In the event you use any of the information in this book for yourself, which is your constitutional right, the author and the publisher assume no responsibility for your actions.

Cover and Book Design by Mark Gelotte, maeric@mac.com

CD produced by Steve Weist, International Sound Studio, isstevew@earthlink.net

Printed in the United States of America

First Edition

Library of Congress Cataloging-in-Publication Data

Sandella, Deborah L.
    Releasing the inner magician : ways to find a peaceful and happy life /
Deborah L. Sandella. -- 1st ed.
    p. cm. -- (Inner magician series; v. 1)
    Includes bibliographical references.
    LCCN: 2001090835
    ISBN: 0-9709445-0-0

    1. Self-perception. 2. Self-realization. 3. Visualization.
    4. Meditation. 5. Spiritual life.
    I. Title.

BF697.5.S43S36 2002   158.1'2
QBI01-201300

TABLE OF CONTENTS

For my dad, Louie Sandella, whose love I carry with me always.

Dearest Reader

Does the voice of your heart long to sing? Come with me and step into your stillness. You will be able to hear the authentic echoes of your inner voice. Faint at first, the whispers will gradually become louder and stronger. The voice you will hear is that of your true nature and is undeniable. The purpose of this book is to raise the volume of your intuitive voice, the inner magician that enchants, illuminates and creates.

When I moved into the tornado belt in Topeka, Kansas as a nine-year-old, I remember being awakened from sleep by hail crashing violently against the metal roof of our mobile home. Even more deafening was the thundering that echoed in my chest. My family and I stared through steamy windows and torrents of rain at a river of lights. Fearful of being left behind, we waded through rising water to our car to join the exodus.

We disappeared into a caterpillar line of cars hoping they would lead us to safety. As it turned out, our haven from the wind and rain was the local reserve armory. The small girl across the road, however, did not fare so well. During her attempt to follow the others, her slight four-year-old body was swept away by the swirling water and found two days later in the creek at the bottom of the hill.

Sometimes, I think I lived much of my life looking with a fearful eye through a steamy window. With one eye fixed toward others, I knew their feelings better than my own and my spirit roamed in search of *home*.

My vision was brought back to center through a dramatic life experience. Thank goodness it was an occurrence of joy and not sorrow as it might have been. Amid banana trees and rainbow-colored parrots, I spent a year with my husband and children on a personal sabbatical, separated from work, friends, extended family and the America familiar. Unplugged from my all-too-familiar world of achieving, comparing and pleasing, I stood out distinctly against the

Australian backdrop like a firefly in the summer night.

I saw *myself* as if for the first time. Naked without my roles and reputation, I beheld a middle-aged woman who had been fooling herself into thinking she was free. My life passed before me like a movie in time-lapse speed, and I realized that while pedaling furiously on my treadmill of doing, I ran constantly in search of others' approval.

Born into an era of feminism and capitalism, I diligently went about earning my worth by acquiring a doctorate degree, a husband, two children, a flourishing psychotherapy practice, a home, two cars and a non-shedding dog. There is nothing wrong with creating these wonderful fruits of life, and I cherish them. There is a distinction, however, in enjoying them rather than employing them as down payments on a self-esteem account that is always lacking.

I've thought of myself as independent-minded and self-aware. At times, I've even considered myself self-actualized. Yet living on the other side of the world, I relearned the ancient teaching—*things are not always as they appear.* As a fish is indifferent to its surrounding water, I had become blind to the sea of busyness that encased me and created a roar that drowned out the inner voice existing in my depths.

Without adornment of professional or social status, I took a free fall into the deepest journey of Self I have ever experienced. For the first time in my life, I truly let myself "be." Life would never be the same. Although this transformation caused me to change many aspects of my existence, I never felt so at home.

I closed my practice of twenty-three years, an inconceivable choice in the past, and found new professional avenues that support a more relaxed lifestyle. Revitalized by this change, I've had the energy to nourish my relationships with Self and family as never before.

By writing this book, I have become a scout. Like the Indian guides of the Old West, I have ventured ahead to explore the territory and map those paths that connect with the inner voice. After all, we teach what we need to learn. Each of the following meditations have grown out of my personal experiences. I lovingly offer them to you with the greatest hope they will take you directly to the fountain of unconditional love that naturally flows from your heart.

The path of self-discovery can be very exciting as you learn to stand in the mystery of life. Knowing your intimate truth makes the days more enjoyable and less stressful. Life becomes a gentle river upon which you can follow your natural flow and determine your way with conviction and ease.

You needn't venture around the world. This book is a safari into the wilds of your own heart. You are about to embark upon a heartfelt journey into your precious center. I invite you to gaze into the shimmering reflection of your soul and drink of the magic.

With Deepest Regard,

Deborah

No journey carries one far unless, as it extends into the world around us,
it goes an equal distance into the world within.
Lillian Smith, The Journey (1954)

———

A Safari Into the Wilds of Your Heart

Prepare to embark upon a journey. You are traveling into your personal heartland, the inner spaces that harbor thoughts and feelings that exist out of your intellectual awareness, an untamed territory. By way of four elemental initiations, you will remember what has been forgotten, release the unnecessary and embrace the essential. This pilgrimage to your inner lands will nourish you in ways the outer world cannot, for it will feed your soul.

The transforming power of self-discovery lies in understanding our true nature, standing in our wholeness and claiming our divinely given powers. The physical body mirrors our humanity, while our inner essence is born of our invisible spirit, heart and soul. Each human being is a unique expression of sacred beauty and soulful humanity. Learning to balance these elements of the Self with respect is a life long challenge.

The journey that lies in front of you will sow seeds of self-understanding that will grow into self-esteem. You will learn how to shift your center of gravity from the external, material world to its rightful home in your invisible, inner landscape. The meditations and exercises will guide you in ways that will help you establish a sense of personal authority. Free to gaze into the *looking glass* of your own reflection, you will discover who you really are. Growing strong with the consistent practice of inner listening, you will stand tall in your inner beauty and power. The true evolution of spirit is to be able to live your personal wisdom, even in the face of dissent.

We frequently shy away from claiming our humanness and imperfections because they tap into the universal fear of unworthiness or of not being good enough. Other times, we just hope we can trick Mother Nature and avoid the pain of experience. We play hide-and-seek, hoping we can fool ourselves into feeling okay.

The heart, however, is not easily tricked, and it quickly creates a storehouse for the pain and guilt we have denied over the years. In the language of the soul, all feelings hold the same value. When we shut off the flow of feelings to resist pain and sorrow, the feelings of love and joy automatically shut off as well. The inner voice falls silent.

In the universe there is, however, a natural intelligence. Regardless of what we label this creative force, it is greater than ourselves and always available to tend our human wounds. It is a fountain of unconditional love.

Proof of this natural wisdom is visible all around us, vividly reflected in our physical world. The tiny, fluttering, ruby-throated hummingbird knows how to find its way to and fro across thousands of miles between North and South America; millions of salmon swim miles upstream to mate and give birth. We cannot look upon any aspect of nature without seeing an inner knowing that wisely evolves life.

Within our mind and body, this intelligence also lives. Nowhere does the natural wisdom express itself more beautifully than in the sacred miracle of birth. The revered philosopher and poet, Ralph Waldo Emerson, pointed out that as creatures of nature, we hold within ourselves the same beauty and perfection that unfolds in physical nature. The same profound essence beating in our heart shapes an intricately patterned snowflake from a raindrop or transforms an awkward, chubby caterpillar into a magnificently graceful butterfly. We are all children of the universe.

To connect with this universal grace and wisdom, you merely need to listen for it in the voice of your intuition. Your divinely endowed spirit provides the exact remedy for the foibles of being human by balancing the resentment, rage, depression and envy with its natural expressions of peace, wisdom and joy. The journey inward allows you to embrace your wholeness, weaving your divine birthright with your human inheritance.

You may sometimes fear that owning your inner beauty is an act of egotism, but to truly see your oneness with the world's magnificence is to feel the unbridled love that is abundantly available for you and for those with whom you walk. As William Blake wrote:

> *To see the world in a grain of sand*
> *And Heaven in a wild flower*
> *Hold infinity in the palm of your hand*
> *And eternity in an hour.*

You can blend your sacred and human echoes into a sweet serenade. Your unique melody is a reflection of your divinely human nature. The meld of divine essence and human nature is magical. The eight sessions described in these two volumes of *Releasing the Inner Magician* attune you to this miraculous rhythm.

Studying physical nature makes visible the heart of our true human and spiritual nature. Core elements of life from which we arose and to which we will return are earth, air, water and fire.

Just as ancient initiates aspired to higher levels of consciousness by interacting with these elements, you will encounter initiations with each.

In session one, you will ground yourself with the element of *earth* as you dig into your many layers. Excavating the artifacts of childhood, adolescence and adulthood, you will reclaim your past as part of your personal evolution.

The element of *air* is felt in session two as you follow your breath down into your heart to heal old wounds.

In session three, you will call home those aspects of yourself that you unconsciously orphaned as the element of *water* provides a metaphor for bathing in pools of forgiveness.

The element of *fire* teaches how to tend your inner fire in session four, as you learn what feeds your passion and what drowns your inner flame.

The essence of who we are, Spirit and Soul, is written with invisible ink. To tap this core of creation, we must allow it to become visible or audible. We will amplify it the way a stethoscope allows us to hear our own heartbeat.

The journey outlined in the following chapters is designed to turn up the volume of your own echoes. Although the meditations anchor each initiation, other tools are employed, creating a variety of channels for learning. Each initiation with *Earth, Air, Water* and *Fire* uses these tools of discovery; there are specific pages at the end of each session for you to record your findings. The four methods employed in each session are described below and include: *intuitive meditations, journal writing, soulful moments* and *metaphoric insights*.

Intuitive Meditations

The voice on the enclosed CD will guide you into your inner magician—the intuitive Self. You will sail the inner passage to heart where truth, power and magic live. The recording will invite your unconscious to bring pictures into your mind's eye. Pictures and feelings comprise the primary and primal language of the body. Children identify pictures from as early as nine months, while the identification of words comes years later.

Visualizing provides an easily accessible corridor to your inner spaces because it shifts your attention to the right brain, the door to the unconscious where you tuck away lost aspects of your Self. Within your mind's eye, you can uncover and communicate with that which hides outside your awareness. The mere act of illumination creates insight. Such clarity highlights appropriate choices and helps you determine whether action is needed.

The act of visualization varies for each individual depending upon one's primary channel for processing information. For example, a visual learner most often sees vivid images, an auditory learner hears voices and a kinesthetic learner feels or senses the picture and its unfolding secrets. There is no right or wrong way to do the following meditations; it is an intuitive trail you follow. Therefore, let your mind's eye guide you.

An Introduction

The following experiment will let you dip into the waters of your mind. In the coming chapters, you will have the opportunity to get immersed, but this experiment takes only a few minutes. Read it first, and then try it.

Start by relaxing your body. Once you are more comfortable, let your eyes close. Invite the image of a television set to appear in your mind. With your inner sight, see or sense your hand turning on the TV. As you watch the screen, see the picture enlarge from a small white spot into a full color picture of your favorite television program.

If distracting images intrude, there are several techniques for clearing out noise. Imagine stacking all extraneous thoughts and concerns to the side to clear space in which to work, trusting that you can bring them back at any time.

Another method is to see each intrusive thought or image being tied to a balloon and floating out of sight beyond the horizon. Similarly, you can float the intruding thoughts and images out of sight on a gently flowing imaginary river.

As your mind becomes clear, picture a family album on a coffee table in front of the television. Notice what the album looks like. Let the book fall open to an image that recorded a happy event from any time in your life. Take a few minutes to let your unconscious go through the pages and find such a picture.

As this specific memory is recalled, notice what thoughts and feelings stir in you.

Does it contain photos from your childhood family, or the family you have created as an adult, or both?

If you wish, you can flip the "on" switch and the picture becomes a video; the scene comes alive. You can watch from a distance, like a director sitting off to the side, observing yourself and others engaged in this event, or you can move your awareness into your figure on the screen and become part of the story. Take a few minutes to enjoy the happiness of this scene then let the image fade and bring your awareness back to the room.

Intuitive images arising from the heart are usually felt very intensely; they reflect your purest inner spirit and therefore nurture your soul. The Australian Aborigines have been visiting the *Dreamtime* for almost 50,000 years. The *Dreamtime* is the stream of consciousness from which creation flows.

Emotion fuels this magic within the mind. When you abandon cerebral thinking and your physical body then look through the eye of your imagination, you can connect directly with your creative inner magician. The following example describes how self-impressions seen during guided/intuitive imagery resulted in breathtaking experiences for participants at *Inner Magician Workshops*.

Kathleen celebrated her fiftieth birthday by attending one of these workshops and shared with the group her experience with the "Into the Heart of the Matter" meditation.

Gently moving into her mind's eye, Kathleen opened an imaginary door to her heart and was awe-struck by her inner beauty. An expansive, vivid green pasture with tall, strong oak trees and sunny, clear skies filled the horizon. The experience represented much more than viewing a pastoral landscape. This imagery was profound because Kathleen was witnessing herself.

Kathleen gazed into the meadow of her inner calm, tasted the richness of her fertility and felt touched by her simple beauty. She saw her spiritual essence without the human filter of self-consciousness. Her inner depths became visible. Later, she wrote, "This image of heart will sustain me for the rest of my life."

Because of your uniqueness, your mind draws intuitively from your bank of images to create an experience that is personally transforming. Having created a gateway to your inner voice, your heart and soul will speak profoundly, raising issues, feelings and constrictions you are ready to break through.

A healthy ego is very protective. If engaged in spontaneous, free-flowing imagery, the unconscious will exercise its right to censure images from entering your awareness until you are ready to process them. When the timing is right, they will be communicated.

For example, the same heart imagery that inspired pastoral images for Kathleen surfaced an old wound for Lena. Although Lena had attended a weekend retreat several years ago, she was not ready to confront her scarred heart landscape at that time, probably because her life was consumed with raising her daughter. Her arrival into an empty nest, however, created the space and energy for the inner listening that offered Lena profound healing.

Lena is a brilliant woman with deep brown eyes and eloquent speech. Her cheerful countenance hid any traces of the grief and sorrow that exploded in her life sixteen years ago when her husband died. Nevertheless, Lena found it necessary to turn her attention to raising their two-year-old daughter, no matter the pain she felt inside.

During the "Into the Heart of the Matter" meditation, Lena began an intense emotional journey. In her mind's eye, she saw spontaneous images of a boat floating on waves. Navigating through the canals of her heart, she sighted a huge, thick scar that rose up in front of the chamber entrance and immobilized her progress. Her inner voice began to sigh with emotion as she recognized the wound of her husband's loss.

Here, clearly visible in the walls of her heart, the pain of his death could not be denied. She could not live fully in her heart until she freed herself from her past by reducing the thickened scar that blocked the entrance.

Her resilient spirit brought forth the picture of an imaginary pumice stone that could be used to clean away the scar. Although fearful of tearing her tender heart wall if she aggressively attacked the old pain, she knew she wanted to love and be loved. Gentle cleansing with this porous stone could be controlled; it offered the perfect solution.

Immediately following this imagery, Lena used journal writing to transfer pain from her heart to the page, and she felt healing far beyond what she thought possible. She called within a few weeks to say she was imagining the pumice stone daily, the scar was gradually dissolving and she was starting to feel great.

Six months later, when Lena attended the third retreat, I asked her to find the secret garden in her heart. Watching through her mind's eye, she saw a miniature roto-tiller gently and thoroughly plowing the remaining scar tissue in her heart.

Delicately, Lena planted her husband's favorite tree and filled the remaining garden space with the color and beauty of her favorite flowers. She tearfully shared with the group that these breathtaking flowers metaphorically represented the love and joy she finally was open to nurture and receive.

Pictures in the mind are perceived as reality because they engender a visceral experience, intuitive images not only can materialize old wounds, they also can provide profound healing.

Journal Writing

"Journal writing bridges the inner and outer worlds and connects the paths of action and reflection," says Christina Baldwin in her book that teaches journal writing as a spiritual quest. Writing down your stream of thoughts lets you see all the chatter you've been carrying around inside.

External expression, through voice or writing, empties the clutter. To gaze upon the written version is to realize that these thoughts and feelings are transient states passing through you, but they are not you. You are much more than your feelings, and emptying them onto the page frees you to again feel your vastness.

Whenever I feel an inner churning, I know confusion is muddying my mood. Taking a few minutes to write in my journal, I soon find relief. Last year, I found myself in a power struggle with my daughter. She resisted my every request. Even washing her hair became a battle, and I felt quite inadequate.

To my surprise, my unconscious leaked into a writing assignment for a poetry class, and seeing a tiny china teacup harvested a deeper understanding. Although much of my journal writing is mundane, this cherished journal entry took me into my heart and brought great insight. It was written about my daughter and to her.

Journal Entry, July 28

A tiny, rounded vessel with a hand-painted blue flower rests on a barn-wood table. The rim where lips have touched and drank tea narrows into a leprechaun-sized handle made for small digits sticky with marmalade jelly. Fingers that search out every hole and corner hoping to find hidden treasure—old jewelry or forgotten sweets—cherished trinkets as reflected in the gleeful eye of childhood.

If only we could sit together, pouring tea and laughing. Of all that is in my care, she is the most precious. Yet, I let my vision wander to trivial tasks, domestic chores and half-written books. Meanwhile, my tea party chair remains vacant.

Sometimes I wish I were in someone else's body, escaping these fears. I would play trickster and tickle them from the inside out, making them giggle without knowing why. And when they were busy at work, I would make their feet itch so badly that they had to get up and walk away from their obsession.

They'd never have a quiet moment because I would be there to knock at their heart, reminding them of my presence, always ready for a new joke or a reckless game. I would be so close to them that sharing the same skin wouldn't be enough; inhabiting their entire being would be my wish. The chatter and tug-of-war would tell me who I am and that I am.

Ahh! Is wanting to get under my skin what her seven-year-old ego seeks? Hitting up again my resistance, she can learn her boundaries, see her ability to spar, to excite, to stir.

Little one, you own my heart, and yet I claim my body. What a mixed message that must seem. You see me as capable, full of confidence, always getting my way, juxtaposed against your childlike lack of knowing.

I, too, have childlike fears and lacks. I, too, am searching out myself amid the experiences of the world. Can you not see me as you pester me from the inside out? Of course you don't, for I don't wish that. The freedom to discover, without interference, is the gift I hope to offer.

I am you and you are me; how can I wrench myself out of the picture without somehow abandoning you? We come together in total union and complete conflict as you worm your way from inside me out into the light of your own, separate life.

We sit together laughing and sipping tea from a small, magic teacup hand-painted with a blue flower.

When I wrote the above journal entry, my childlike self showed her face and spontaneously connected with my daughter's playful and evolving seven-year-old ego. How freeing it felt to appreciate her humor and her spirit. My anger and guilt dissolved as I vividly re-experienced the love-hate relationship inherent in separation. You probably have guessed that our relationship improved immensely after I lightened up.

Personal writing is an intimate expression. The page holds the most intense pain and rage without complaint. Pure expression without critique—what a pleasure! The unconditional acceptance of a journal is a great teacher. As you unravel your feelings with your journal as witness, you learn unconditional love for the fragile, inner spirit that fears abandonment or rejection.

Journal writing is one of the greatest gifts we can give ourselves. It provides a blank page upon which to project. Unlike a human listener, the journal has no hidden insecurities that can cloud the projection. Without opposition or others' agendas crowding you, you can write until your personal truths float to the top, like cream rising to the surface.

Stream-of-consciousness writing also can be a lightning rod to connect with the divine within you. As your writing takes you beneath the chatter and garbage, you will hear another voice—it is the sound of your inner magician or the divine inner voice. Some call it the higher self or the God within.

When my writing naturally transitions from complaints, anger and noise into words of compassion for myself and others, I know it has been successful. Great insight can be accessed at this point in time.

In fact, you can write an interactive interview with your God Self to connect with a divine perspective on your problems. Personally, I have found this method to be very helpful in bringing forth inspired answers. Similar to Neale Donald Walsch's writings in the *Conversations with God* book series, you can dialogue with the God within. Write down your questions and then let God's response write itself through you.

The journal-writing exercises outlined in each coming session are designed to help you remember and integrate the insights uncovered in the meditations. Reading what you have written at a later time will allow you to savor the delicious experience again, as well as see new truths. The vivid nature of imagery, like a powerful dream, seems so real that it can never be forgotten, and, like a dream, the passion fades in the light of ordinary life and becomes lost all too quickly. Keeping a record of these thoughts, feelings and insights will keep them forever available to you.

Some sessions contain written exercises with a specific purpose. With both the journal and exercise questions, please write freely without editing or critiquing. Write whatever comes, and keep writing until your mind is empty.

You may wish to begin daily journal writing if you aren't already doing so. To connect daily with the inner voice is clarifying as well as freeing. Julia Cameron, author of *The Artist's Way*, suggests readers empty their minds of all the chatter that's eating up the precious inner space so they can connect with the Creative Self.

Soulful Moments

To deepen your experience, please look for a soulful moment hidden in each week. Each initiation with *Earth, Air, Water* and *Fire* will have space for you to record these experiences on the pages at the end of the session. The following discussion explains *soulful moments* so that you can recognize them.

Soulful moments are those times when you open your heart to the beauty and wholeness of nature, and you know the preciousness of your own vulnerability. For that moment in time, you merge with the pulse of life and revel in its power. There are many avenues to soulful moments such as nature, music/dance, playfulness and human connection. These examples are described below.

NATURE

The natural world offers many visual touchstones that open the heart. Iridescent dawns and burning sunsets are but two examples in nature when the magnificence of the universe shines through.

One of my most soulful moments happened during my daily run when I lived in Australia. On one particular day, I was in a real funk about the weather because we were deluged with the wettest, coldest winter in their recent history. My vision had been of writing a book while nestled in a warm tropical paradise; my dream became juxtaposed against the cold reality.

Running along and ruminating about the lack of sunshine, I glanced to the horizon. Illuminated against a backdrop of dark, brooding thunderclouds appeared a pair of gargantuan cloud-formed hands. Cupped hands with distinct fingers spiraling upward, the clouds created a large, cushioned space—a sanctuary.

Like a broken bird with a twisted wing that senses rescue, my worried mind propelled me into this skyward respite. My imaginary body relaxed into weightlessness and freedom. Running and playing, I danced and twirled with abandon. Feeling loved and sheltered, I felt a visceral wave of unconditional acceptance sweep through me. It brought tears.

In the light of this heavenly caress, worry drained away, and I began to "see" that the winter's rain had actually pushed me to write. Sunny days offered up many enticements, but wet weather kept me close to the computer. I collected and polished this image and put it away with my treasured memories recorded in my journal. This ever-so-gentle holding has supported me through many obsessive worries.

Music and Dance

Music, the language of the soul, also opens your heart and helps you connect inward. As Victor Hugo so poignantly said, "Music expresses that which cannot be said and on which it is impossible to be silent." Take a minute to listen to music with your heart and see the results.

An "explosive expression of humanity" is how singer Billy Joel described music; dancing is similar. Since the beginning of time, people have used dance as a way to connect with the gods, to express themselves and to empower their rituals.

You can dance your soul home by tuning into the rhythm of your own liveliness. Feel the music and let your body push through any inhibitions and move freely. Like the unfettered joy of a child's singing and dancing, your pure spirit, full of energy and power, can overflow and fill the room.

Childlike Playfulness

To seek the child within is to remember your original joy in living. This week, my now nine-year-old daughter reminded me of the great pleasure that comes from looking through eyes of wonder. Discovering the first, thin blanket of snow outside her window, she exclaimed, "Mom, it's a dream come true!" Her delight made my adult trepidation about the coming of winter seem dull by comparison.

Open yourself to spontaneous moments of playfulness and curiosity, and feel the mask of adulthood fall away. Let the veil of civilized appearances part, and invite your witty, soulful Self to spill buckets of laughter and tears!

HUMAN CONNECTION

Poignant moments of connection with others offer additional opportunities for soulful moments. At times when you authentically soften your edges, you connect in love. Such encounters need not be romantic to be exquisite. A few years ago, I experienced a profound soulful moment as I connected with my father who lay unconscious in the hospital following a cardiac arrest.

Sitting at his bedside in the darkness of night, it was as if he and I were the only two people in the world. Speaking to him aloud, I shared my feelings of love and gratitude. This soulful coming together led me to forgive him for all the mistakes he made as a father and to realize how little they mattered in light of his unfailing love.

His physical condition provided the opportunity to connect as his equal, rather than as his daughter. This realignment changed our relationship forever. Following this time together, my father recovered his health, and we recovered a precious connection.

Also, *soulful moments* emerge when we embrace humanity by supporting others who are in pain. Compassion reminds us of our mortality, and we deepen our gratitude. How often we hear stories of lasting memories created between those who have bonded in the midst of difficult situations like combat, graduate school or the illness or death of a loved one. The connection transpires again in the telling of a heart-breaking or heart-warming story. Storyteller and listener link hearts.

Allowing yourself to slow down and become aware of your feelings will lead you naturally to grace, a place of clarity where you can feel the soul of the world. When you connect with the spirit of all living things, you flood your heart with feelings of compassion. Enraptured in that crystalline moment, insights flow naturally from the depths of your soul.

Emerson captured this thought eloquently,

> *. . . within man is the soul of the whole; the wise silence; the universal beauty, to which every part and particle is equally related; the eternal ONE. And this deep power in which we exist and whose beatitude is all accessible to us, is not only self-sufficing and perfect in every hour, but the act of seeing and the thing seen, the seer and the spectacle, the subject and the object, are one. We see the world piece by piece, as the sun, the moon, the animal, the tree; but the whole, of which these are the shining parts, is the soul.*

The exercises in this book will help you clean the windows to your soul, so you can see clearly these powerful moments tucked within your daily experiences.

Metaphoric Insights

Metaphoric insights, similar to soulful moments, quicken the transformational process and can be recorded on the pages at the end of each initiation session. The following discussion will orient you to them.

Metaphoric thinking grows your understanding by comparing something familiar with something unfamiliar. You look for similarities to give you a new slant on life. For example, Roger Von Oech, in *A Whack on the Side of the Head*, writes wonderful metaphors that help us understand life and demonstrate how each metaphor communicates a different message:

"Life is like a room full of open doors that close as you get older."

"Life is like a puppy dog always searching for a street full of fire hydrants."

During the coming sessions, look at your routine occurrences through metaphoric lenses and search for similarities between your inner and outer workings. If you develop a habit of seeing the messages hidden in your experiences, metaphoric thinking will be one of the most exciting changes you'll ever make. Irritating experiences that you've previously viewed as a waste of time will be transformed into illuminating insights.

The other day, my friend Kelly, feeling totally frustrated, called to say she would be delayed because her car had been "booted." Booting is an inconvenient Denver Police invention that immobilizes a car for non-payment of parking tickets. Kelly, too, was immobilized since she lacked transportation. Much to my surprise, and hers, she called back within minutes to say she was able to free her car from bondage with a brief call to the traffic center where they were happy to take her credit card number to cover parking fees and dispatch a policeman to remove the boot.

As we talked, the metaphor within the experience shined clearly. Stuck in binding relationships with a boyfriend and an overly protective mother, Kelly was engaged in an emotional struggle to extricate herself. The episode with her car was a perfect metaphor. Although the car had been immobilized, she had been able to arrange its release quickly and with little trouble. The insight loomed; the quick, pro-active attitude that freed her car could assure her personal freedom as well!

In the same way you use a thermometer to convey unseen processes occurring inside the body, experiences occurring in our immediate external field can mirror inner dynamics. When you use a thermometer to obtain a reading of body temperature, the feedback given does not describe the thermometer but tells you about the body in intimate proximity to the thermometer. Similarly, your immediate external experiences can give you a reading about invisible or unconscious internal conditions, as demonstrated in the story of Kelly's car. External occurrences gave her a reading about her internal immobilization and possible options.

Metaphoric insights can be quite dramatic at times. A dear family friend, Dave, recently navigated a career change. Retiring from his job of twenty-three years as a city planner, he is pursuing his passion—art. A quiet man with conservative ways, Dave's decision took a huge leap of faith.

Not long after saying his final farewells to his officemates, Dave went solo mountain biking in Utah. An experienced biker, he had trekked in Utah for many years. The morning was sunny and warm when he set out for a day of biking on one of the rugged Moab trails. After six hours of riding through dusty terrain, Dave became worried; he felt sure he should be near the end of the trail, yet there was no hint of it. When he came upon a trail-side camper in late afternoon, Dave studied this fellow's detailed map and realized he had mistakenly wandered onto a trail much longer than a day's ride. He decided to turn around expecting that he could reach his car at the trailhead before dark. Black shadows, however, crept over him before he saw the parking lot.

Fearful of hitting a rock or tree, Dave abandoned riding and curled up to keep himself warm. Overwhelmed with sleepiness, he feared that hypothermia was near. With eyes forced open, he sat shivering in the moonlight until glimmers of light eventually signaled dawn. Although he felt exhausted by the night's exposure, he forced his legs to make every rotation as he biked the remaining miles to his car. Physically depleted but emotionally victorious, Dave made a heartfelt call home saying, "I survived. I'm alive." What a powerful metaphor. He survived!

Dave's passion fueled his ability to tolerate exposure to the elements and push through his exhaustion to continue pedaling. His experience, like a thermometer, told him he had the courage to pursue his career change—because he could survive getting lost. Being truly alive is worth risking death.

Whenever we risk exploring the unfamiliar, we must know in our hearts that we can survive getting lost. As French author, Andre Gide, wistfully wrote, "One doesn't discover new lands without consenting to lose sight of the shore for a very long time."

A powerful metaphor hit me up side the head a few years ago when my husband's business was notified that investment funds had been squandered. My Italian temper flared. Like a vigilante, I wanted to hunt down the bandits and make them pay.

Not long after this, while working on the computer, creating mailing labels, I realized, much to my horror, that I had deleted a large data file and faced having to re-enter numerous addresses. Quickly, I called a friend who was a computer consultant and asked him to talk me through retrieval of the deleted file from the computer garbage bin. To make a long story short, my attempts to recover what was lost ended up destroying the mother board. Being computer illiterate at the time, it cost us for repairs and, of course, I had to re-enter all the address data.

Soon the computer was up and running, but don't think this story is about computers. Remember, the thermometer doesn't have a temperature.

When I looked through metaphoric lenses, I found an important insight in this scenario. Trying to recover what was already lost would probably be costly as well as fruitless. Seeing the metaphor brought me an answer I trusted. The best answer to the lost retirement money was to let the mistake go and move forward. Releasing the emotional tension felt totally right when I heeded this metaphoric directive.

Not only is the metaphoric relationship between our inner workings and our external world enlightening, but scientific study has documented that the external world can be influenced by the mind. In his book *Recovering the Soul*, physician and visionary Larry Dossey synthesizes the scientific evolution of relevant physics theory. He suggests that the greatest scientific thinkers of our time agree that our minds are not limited by space and time nor confined to our brains or bodies.

In fact, Robert Jahn and Brenda Dunne in their book, *Margins of Reality*, present research findings demonstrating that humans can psychically influence random physical activities, such as the output of machines and patterns of falling, styrofoam balls.

Several months ago, I found myself facing such an external metaphor. During my morning jog, my new cassette earphones stopped working. "Darn," I thought, "this same problem caused me to throw away two pair of earphones in the last two weeks." Without success, I jiggled the connections, hoping to make contact between the loose wires.

Eventually, the "ah ha" arrived when I realized that buying new ear phones wasn't solving the problem, maybe the problem wasn't in the ear phones, but in my ears. I had avoided this possibility as long as I could, but the resistance to piling up more broken earphones strongly motivated me. I finally reached the point where my desire to have working earphones was greater than my wish to be "right." Considering whether a metaphoric insight might lurk in the space between my ears and the phones, I asked myself, *"Was there something or someone I was not hearing?"*

Not quite ready to abandon my righteousness and admit wrongdoing, I decided to experiment with the concept. I had been tuning out my husband lately because I didn't like his comments, but surely this couldn't cause my earphones to stop working?

Acting as if this were a *metaphoric insight*, I wrote in my journal to gain insight and compassion. Needless to say, I learned a few things about how resistant I was being. Miraculously, after I acknowledged my stubbornness and made amends, full sound returned to my earphones and they have transmitted music flawlessly ever since.

More often, looking through our metaphoric lenses is less dramatic than that instance. For example, Elaine, a beautiful woman whose unlined face glows, recently told of seeing her passage through menopause reflected in a golden oak tree. Navigating the seasons, this grand and stable tree was shedding its vibrant leaves and moving into winter, a time of hibernation. Elaine sensed that as her body was shedding certain functions, she was approaching a new season of life. She felt affirmed when she gazed at this grand tree; she saw the beauty and wisdom of her aging soul and knew that in the natural change of seasons, spring follows winter.

Experiment! Look at your own daily interactions in the world as a reflection of your inner workings and see what you discover. Be open to the possibility that your mind can create changes in the material world, changes that are mirrors of your inner Self and, therefore, experiences from which you can learn. Let the world become your looking glass.

Each of the following four sessions offers a recorded meditation, a journal-writing exercise, a soulful moment activity and a metaphoric insight activity. Move through these initiations at your own pace. Take as much time as you need. They will help you chart the path into your soft center. Remember to enter with a sense of reverence and a willingness to listen. The path of self-discovery, undertaken with commitment, releases the inner magician. Don't be surprised if magic happens!

Be gentle with yourself during the following sessions. If at any time you need personal psychological support, please contact a counselor or therapist. Referrals can be obtained from friends or your health care practitioner. Also, the Academy for Guided Imagery has a list of therapists around the country who are certified in the use of Interactive Guided Imagery. They can be reached at 1-800-726-2070.

Traveling Companions

An especially effective way to travel this journey of self-exploration is in the company of a small group that meets regularly. In the safety of each other's presence, you can discover the inward path. Discussion can illuminate and cement the shared and individual insights. You will only trust your inner voice once you have used it with others. Keeping it secret will support a belief that you will not be accepted if you show your true colors.

When I left Australia at the end of our sabbatical, I didn't understand the extreme sadness I felt after leaving our short-term friends. At home, my life had many lifelong relationships, yet this farewell felt as if my heart was breaking.

As time softened the ache, clarity settled in, and I saw that because I wore my true nature from the beginning, my Australian friends saw me in a light that others rarely were allowed. Great healing lived in the experience of being loved without the filter of trying to please. The fear of rejection that bound me to pleasing others was lifted.

Only in the experience of baring myself could I trust that I was lovable. Out of this insight came the energy to expose my feelings with lifelong friends, and telling the truth has become easier. Although I relapse at times, I savor the feeling of *being good enough just as I am*. If you seek an opportunity to share your inner spirit with others, consider undertaking this journey of self-discovery with a group.

Even if you choose to go solo, I encourage you to experiment by speaking from your heart with others. You'll learn to trust yourself by risking exposure and surviving. Eventually, you must be able to claim your uniqueness without compromising your spirit.

If you are seeking a group, Rollene Saal makes useful suggestions for starting one in her book, *The New York Public Library Guide to Reading Groups*. She suggests inviting three friends who would be interested and ask them each to invite one other person. Since *Releasing the Inner Magician* involves self-disclosure, suggest to others that they invite people who are trustworthy and capable of maintaining confidentiality. Set the ground rules during the first meeting and respect them. Housekeeping items could include such details as confidentiality, facilitator rotation, meeting times, location, frequency, food or no food and meeting flow.

If the group finds it needs more assistance, consider inviting a therapist or counselor to facilitate.

Fossicking

During my time in Australia, I learned that many precious stones are rumored to have spent millions of years creeping their way up through the earth's crust seeking a day in the sun. Tourists love to go "fossicking." With pick in hand, they travel the ground and cliffs of the natural gem fields in search of the occasional sapphire, diamond or garnet.

Like a fossicker, dig into the earth of your soul. Illumined by the flame of your heart, you will find in the stream of your consciousness the treasured gem that glistens within.

Happy hunting!

"Man's psyche is as infinite within as
the universe is without."
Carl Jung

———

An Initiation with Earth

Digging into the soil of my past,
I prepare the garden of my future.

Earth is but a tiny part of the huge universe, yet it is home to a multitude of humans, animals and plants. Over 4.3 billion years old, her many sediment layers are etched with stories of the past. Engraved within these strata are fossils and traces of her history and origins. Piecing this information together like a puzzle, geologists understand the evolutionary mysteries of the ages.

Like the earth, we have many layers that have evolved over a lifetime. As we age, our depth and history accumulate. We, too, can uncover our earthy layers and appreciate our archeology. Remembering the fossils of our past experiences, we can integrate who we have been and who we are becoming.

This session will guide you in several ways. Initially, you will dig down through your adult, adolescent and child layers to integrate your past. Once you are deep in your center, you will visit the secret garden of your soul where you will weed out unnecessary thoughts, feelings and behaviors; then you'll plant new seeds for future manifestation.

By bravely digging through the callused exterior layers, you can reconnect with the awe of your divinely human nature. Deep in your center beneath the fear, doubt and unworthiness is the seed of your original wholeness. Here lives the light of your inner essence.

Roots grow from this essential core and connect you with your family of origin. Growing through the years, new sprouts have taken you in unique directions. Although these roots are very much a part of your whole, you never lose the opportunity for creating new sources of nourishment and stability. Some roots shrink and whither while others flourish. Awareness of your roots can help nurture those that move you in desirable directions and help identify those that must be plucked.

Just as the earth continues in its natural adaptation, we, too, grow and change. Wondrously, as we develop insight about our natural growth process, we can plant new seedlings to grow us in the direction of our physical, psychological and spiritual destiny.

During the upcoming meditation, you will have the opportunity to trek down into your earthy layers, witness your roots and tend the garden of your soul. Barbara traced such a journey during an *Inner Magician* workshop when the memory of her adolescent Self brought insight into a current conflict.

Barbara was becoming increasingly short-tempered with her thirteen-year-old son. A single mother since he was three, her patience was wearing thin as she listened weekly to his teacher's complaints about his disruptive antics in class.

When Barbara attended the workshop in search of a solution, she had no idea that her answer lay in the cracks of time—her own adolescence—a time of extreme loneliness. In contrast, her popular son was willing to do anything, including misbehave, in order to make his friends laugh. Entertaining his peers ranked at the peak of his priorities and was the primary source of his school problems.

She immediately felt a softening of her anger as she recalled her own excruciating pain. In fact, she discovered that she was proud of her son because he was able to make and keep friends; he was succeeding where she had failed.

In weeding out unnecessary anger and fear, Barbara lovingly reconnected with her son. Although limit-setting was still necessary, she described feeling very different. Empathy displaced her rage. Two months later, she told me her son's behavior had turned a significant corner.

Journal Exercise

for Integrating Your Roots

To respect your history is to acknowledge your inherent strength. Fantasize for a minute what the earth would be like if it were hollow rather than layered. Merely a shell, it would risk collapse. Similarly, when we try to extract our history, we feel empty. In the coming exercises, you have the opportunity to illuminate a spiritual tunnel to your soul and shed light on your origins. Look with new eyes for the resilience and insight arising from the ashes of your past and claim your wholeness with compassion!

Give yourself plenty of time and write spontaneously to empty your reservoir of feelings. There is wisdom contained in both your intuitive first association and in digging deeper into underlying layers. Look through your mind's eye to envision the brief meditation, then answer the following questions to help you integrate the roots you formed long ago. Or did they form you?

Close your eyes briefly and envision your childhood home. Walk into your bedroom and notice what you see and feel. Walk around, from room to room, until you locate your parents. Notice how they look and how you feel as you greet them. When you are ready, open your eyes and begin answering the following questions.

The place I felt most safe as a child was. . .

The place I felt least safe as a child was. . .

In grade school, I had the most fun when . . .

The taste of _____ always reminds me of . . .

What I loved most about my best friend was . . .

I hated _____ because I felt . . .

My worst moment in childhood was. . .

because I felt . . .

Out of this experience, I have come to believe that . . .

I was the happiest when . . .

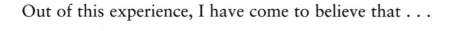

Out of this experience, I have come to believe that . . .

My mother viewed life as . . .

The burden I inherited because of her world view was . . .

The gift I inherited because of her world view was . . .

My father viewed life as . . .

The burden I inherited as a result of his world view was . . .

The gift I inherited because of his world view was . . .

Around my siblings I felt . . .

In my family, I played the role of . . .

This role is replicated in my life today in these ways . . .

The outcome of replicating these roles is . . .

I have released these roles in the following ways . . .

The outcome of releasing these roles is . . .

The replications from childhood I would like to interrupt are . . .

The following changes would be necessary to accomplish the above . . .

Close your eyes for a minute and see a movie of your life as it would be if you completed the above changes . . .

_____ stops me from making the above changes because . . .

What I have learned about myself from answering these questions is . . .

When I admire a person, the characteristics and behaviors I see are . . .

This person is a mirror of me in these ways . . .

The qualities I wish to nourish are . . .

Go to www.innermagician.com to download journal pages for personal use.

39

Meditation

Unearthing Your Soul

The following meditation has been recorded on track number one of the enclosed CD. There are a variety of ways that you can experience the meditations; feel free to use whatever method works best for you and your style of processing information. Various options include:

- Find a comfortable place to relax, away from others, and let the recorded voice guide you. When you're finished, take out your journal and answer the questions listed at the end of the session.
- Read the written version prior to listening to the recording.
- Read the meditation and freely record your experience in your journal as you proceed through the meditation. Since you can move at your own pace without being distracted by pausing the CD, you can record more detail.
- While reading the meditation, record your experiences on tape rather than in writing.

This meditation will guide you in integrating your memories and feelings and planting new seeds in the garden of your soul.

Intuitive imagery is experienced in a personal way. You may see images, hear sounds or feel sensations or emotions within your imagination or mind's eye. Whatever experience your mind brings is perfect.

If your mind seems to consistently take you in a direction different from the voice on the CD, follow your intuition; this is not distraction but important feedback from your unconscious mind. There's no need to criticize or edit, follow your natural flow and feel free to pause the CD if you need more time.

Find a place where you can relax without being
interrupted for 20-30 minutes. Lower the lights and get
into a comfortable position, either sitting or lying down,
as you begin the journey down through your layers,
digging into the soil of your past and preparing the garden
of your future.
Settle into yourself and allow your eyes to gently close.
With a deep cleansing breath, exhale all tension. Breathe in
relaxation and exhale doubt; breathe in clarity and exhale
confusion. When you are relaxed, turn in to your place of
wisdom. In your mind's eye, invite the image of a place in
nature. It may be someplace you have visited or a place you are
creating in your mind at this moment. Sense the power, beauty
and safety of this place. Breathe it in and let it fill you. As
you relax in this sweet spot, notice the temperature of the air
against your skin, the smells and the sounds.
Taking a deep breath of tranquillity, look around until you
discover a hidden trail. Follow it until it leads you to a
rocky cliff, where, peering over the edge, you see a small dirt
road that crisscrosses along the rocky cliffs to the bottom of
a canyon. Sure-footed, like a mountain goat, find the entrance
to this trail and climb downward.
On the underside of the edge, you discover a small cliff
dwelling. This site houses the fossils of your adult life.
Wander around this place and reclaim valuable information
about your adulthood. Take some time. **What do you find?**
What meaning do these items have for you? Gazing at this site
and its artifacts, feel clarity about the primary lesson that has
consumed your adulthood.

Look around for a container in which you may carry
relics with you during this journey. **What do you see as
you walk down the path? What catches your eye? How
do these objects represent you?** Collect items to represent
your adult nature. Take some time.
Give thanks to your adult Self for the gifts s/he has brought
you and follow the cliff-side trail deeper down into the
canyon. As you round the bend, notice that an older strata
of rock is exposed. This is the strata of your adolescence.
Study this rock wall and the art etched into it to understand
the wisdom it reveals about this time in your life. Take some
time to learn about your inner pubescent Self.
In front of you, bones lie in the graveyard of your adolescence.
Pick them up and feel their energy. **What do you notice?**
As you hold these artifacts, let an image of the adolescent
"you" float into your mind. **What do you look like? What
does your adolescent Self feel like? Ask this image what was
your greatest sorrow during your adolescence? What was
your greatest joy? What does this adolescent Self want you
to know about your adult Self?**
Say a prayer of gratitude to your adolescent, then take these
bones with you as you return to the dirt trail. Follow it
farther down into the canyon. Soon you come upon another
cliff dwelling, one more ancient than the first. It houses the
fossils of your childhood. Walk around and explore this area.
**What are the items, fossils and shards lying about? What
valuable information do they reveal about your inner child?**
Relics from your childhood graveyard lie on the ground.
Collect them to carry with you. **As you touch them, what do**

you discover about your inner child?

Invite an image of your inner child to enter your mind's
eye. **What age does this child appear to be? How is s/he
dressed? What feelings are present?
What role did this child play in your family? How did s/he
feel about this role? How were boundaries handled by your
family?**

**Ask this child what wisdom s/he has to impart to you. What
words did this child long to hear from your parents?** Right
now, say these words. Take a minute.

**How does your inner child continue to cry out in your life?
What does s/he want from you?**

When you are ready, let these images fade. Bless this site and
say a prayer of gratitude to your inner child.

Notice how the area feels and looks. **Has it changed in any way
since you first arrived?**

Begin walking down the dirt trail again. Spiral down deeper
and deeper until you sense a divine aura. There, in your
presence, is the sacred garden of your soul. Find a space of
earth that feels powerful and safe. Let your intuition guide you.
Dig a shallow space large enough for your body.

In this cleared space of earth, arrange your collection of
bones, fossils and shards in the outline of your true nature.
Take some time.

Lie down in this sacred site upon your fossils and say a prayer
of forgiveness. Feel the earth crumble against your skin and
smell the sweet scent of moisture. Allow your tears to flow
freely and water your garden.

Breathing deeply, your hot breath enlivens these relics and

your inner flame melds them into you.

There, deep in your DNA, you feel the seed of your
original wholeness gently being nourished by the wisdom
of your past.

Suddenly, clouds cover the sun, and darkness covers the
earth. A crack of lightning strikes, and you feel the original
electricity of your nature as you fall deep into the center of
your being.

Look around. **What do you see?**

You have fallen into your vastness. Floating in the void,
connect with the Source of all creation. Take some time.

Observe yourself from this place and ask, **"What is the essence
of my inner spirit?"**

Suddenly a lovely voice speaks. It is your inner voice.

Ask, **"What is my greatest gift, that aspect of me that innately
craves to bloom? How is this gift related to my life's
purpose?"** Take a moment to listen.

**"What are the human imperfections that give me depth?
What is my greatest lesson for this lifetime?"**

Listen as the voice shares with you words of wisdom and
encouragement.

Take some time to ask any questions you might have.

When you are ready, feel your essence form itself into a seed.

Nestle into a tender bed of earth and feel yourself swell with
warmth and moisture in preparation for germination. Gently,
crack open and grow new roots to ground you. In your mind's
eye, take some time to grow them as deep and wide as desired.

Once centered in the earth mother, feel a small sprout of Self
peek out, a little green shoot that breaks through the crust of

the ground. Open to receive the nourishing rays of sun
and begin to grow at your own pace. **How do you feel?**
Soak up the sun, and in your own time, feel your inner
spirit burst into full bloom.
What new parts of yourself are unfolding?
How do you feel?
Let yourself become fully ripe. How does this feel?
When you're ready, your ripe bloom dies away into mother
earth and incubates to form a new seed. **What feelings rise
up during this stage?**
Take some time now to flow through the growing process until
your unconscious mind comes to rest in your current stage of
growth. **What stage is this?**
What have you learned about yourself and your growth?
Look around and see what weeds, in the form of thoughts,
behaviors and habits, need to be plucked in order for you to
grow in the direction of your dreams. In your mind's eye,
see those weeds being removed. **How does this feel?**
Take some time.
What have you learned during this meditation?
How can you apply this knowledge in your life?

When you are ready, let your mind journey back to this room.
Become aware of your surroundings. Let your arms and legs
return to their normal weight as you wiggle the feeling back
into your fingers and toes. Take whatever time you need, then
open your eyes and answer the questions on the next page.

Journal Exercise

Unearthing Your Soul

Describe your "cliff dwelling" of adulthood. What did you learn about your nature and your primary lesson as an adult?

What did the rock art and bones of your adolescence teach you about this time in your life? What did your adolescent Self have to say?

What did you learn about your inner child? What words did your inner child crave to hear? For what does s/he still cry out?

What wisdom did the voice of your soul share?

What is your primary lesson for this lifetime? What is your life's purpose?

What is your greatest gift that longs to blossom? How is it connected with your life's purpose?

What was your experience as a seed germinating into a flower? How is this similar to your life experience?

What parts of you are blossoming at this time in your life?

What parts of you are germinating in preparation for full bloom?

What was your experience as a ripe bloom dying and returning to the earth for rebirth?

Currently, in what stage of the growing cycle are you?

Please journal freely any additional insights or experiences.

Go to www.innermagician.com to download journal pages for personal use.

53

Soulful Moment

Activity Suggestion

Take a meditative walk in nature making each step a conscious connection between your feet and the earth. Remember to breathe deeply and fully and notice the earth energy that comes up through the "souls" of your feet. Pay attention to the feeling of this energy in different locations and different kinds of terrain. Look at the surface of the ground. Observe closely the plants, insects, leaves, rocks, etc. as you pass. Stop and touch them if you feel the urge. If possible, watch the sun set and notice its departing imprint. Record your experiences below.

or

Record a spontaneous Soulful Moment. You may want to refer to the *Introduction* on page 16 for a detailed description.

My Soulful Moment was _____ when I felt:

Metaphoric Insight

Activity Suggestion

While you are on your meditative walk, hold a question for which you seek an answer in your mind. Find a rock that catches your attention. Hold it in your hand. Ask the question and let the formations, cracks and irregularities on each side of the rock be a metaphor for your answer. Be open to the new! Record your findings below.

or

Record a spontaneous Metaphoric Insight. You may want to refer to the *Introduction* for a detailed definition.

My Metaphoric Insight was _____ when I felt:

Record the Wisdom Gleaned from Your Initiation with EARTH

Record the primary lessons learned from this session's meditation/journaling/soulful moment/metaphoric insight. Use words and images freely as your imagination directs.

Ways I can incorporate this knowing into my life:

1.

2.

3.

Earth cradles me as I integrate my many layers.
Anchored by solid roots, I grow out of the
kernel of my original wholeness
into the me I was born to be.
I smile gratitude.

———

An Initiation with Air

Air, enter my waiting body
and teach me about receiving and letting go.
Let your rise and fall remind me of the natural expansion
and constriction of life.
Bless me now as
I swing on a breath.

Air is an illusory element that covers land and sea and extends far above the earth's surface, yet it remains invisible. We cannot see, smell or taste air, but it is as real as wood and fire.

Moving air can be seen in the effects of drifting clouds, pounding waves and trembling leaves. The power of air can explode in destructive hurricanes and tornadoes, yet also be as gentle as caresses blown by summer breezes. This session's initiation with air teaches the subtle yet immense power of the invisible forces.

Air is life itself. People have lived without water for a week, but without air we can survive only a few minutes. Our life swings on each breath. With each inspiration we choose to live, and with each expiration there is a death of the passing moment.

The true significance of breathing flashed before me recently when a fellow traveler collapsed at the airport a few feet from where I stood. Hovering with the small circle of others who rushed to help, my pulse raced at the recognition of his stalled heartbeat and his purple, motionless face. Sitting near his right shoulder, I supported his neck as another passenger gave him her breath through CPR. His lifeless blue-gray eyes bulged frozen in a look of pure panic. All signs of life vacated; only an empty body of flesh remained.

Would spirit and matter reunite? Would his breath spontaneously flow again? When I asked his friend, who stood at my left shoulder, to communicate with the body before us, I was moved to tears as he spoke. "Bill, buddy, this is John. Bill, you are okay. Everything is going to be all right. I'm here with you, buddy. Stay with me."

Warm, caring recognition by a friend transformed a lifeless body into a man named Bill. In response, there came a subtle communion between spirit and body. Somewhere in the universe, where souls hover, a reunion was courted. As if considering the friend's invitation, Bill's contorted face softened. Suddenly, I felt the shift; an empty body became occupied. The purple faded.

Paramedics arrived shortly and returned Bill's heartbeat with two, swift electric charges to the chest. Bill was carried away to the hospital. The blip of the heart monitor sounded a normal beat and an IV dripped into receptive veins. In those few minutes, the relationship between life and breath was illumined against a backdrop of death.

Our bodies allow us to experience the mortal world. They register pleasure and pain, and they collect information through our senses, sensations and feelings. Yet it is the immortal soul that enlivens us on wings of breath.

Breathing is a constant reminder of the transient union of spirit and body that is life. The rhythm of exhale upon inhale helps us remember there is only the present moment. Become conscious of your breath and increase your awareness of being alive.

New Mexico poet Nancy Wood, writes soulfully of this connection.

Connections

Every time we take a breath, we become
    the universe. The very moment of creation
is contained in us and passes on to rocks and trees,
    animals and fish. The old ones say the essence of life
is in water and wind, earth and breath, fire and bone,

but most of all in breath, our first connection
to the elk, the hawk, the bear, and the buffalo.
Without breath, no connection.
Without connection, no creation.
Without creation, no breath.
This is the sacred circle of life, unbroken.

Take a deep breath now and feel it flow within you. Exhale
deeply. Then let your next inhale travel all the way down to
your toes. What do you notice?
First of all, you may notice you have toes. So much of our day
is spent preoccupied that we sometimes lose contact with our
physical bodies. Notice sensations in your body as you
consciously slow your breath. Where do you notice tension
or tightness?
Return your awareness to your breathing, flowing with
everything that passes in, then passes away.
Let yourself swing on each breath. As your chest and abdomen
expand, see yourself swinging upward. When you reach the
natural peak, begin a gentle descent on the wings of your
exhale. Gliding forward on each in-breath, let your heart
behold the world around you and expand in rhythm with
your chest.

Gracefully swinging backwards, release your breath to
the sky so you may be filled again. Ride your breath for
a few minutes.

When you're ready, sit with your feet flat on the floor and
your lower back against a chair or wall. If you wish, you
may close your eyes.

Take three long breaths. Exhale deeply each time. Focus
your attention on your breathing without changing it.
Just become aware of it.

Relax further continuing to focus on your breathing. Notice
the precise point at which your breath starts to come in and
starts to go out.

Without changing anything except your attention, act as if the
air is breathing you. Give up control of your breathing.
Surrender. Let the air be the doer; let it reach into you and
draw itself out.

Now, reverse your point of view and act as if you are the
doer. Observe yourself as the one doing the breathing.
Now shift once again, and act as if the air is breathing you.
This time notice if there is any change in your feelings when
you shift from the controlling role to the surrendering role.
Switch again. Act as if you are breathing the air and you are
in the controlling role. Notice the change in feeling.
Relax and think for a moment about the differences you
observed in the two kinds of breathing experiences.

Breathing reminds us of the natural rhythm of life, the ebb and flow that is the nature of being human. Take time each day to become conscious of your breathing. Let the continuous coming in and going out keep you aware of your vibrancy.

When we cling to the passing moment expressed in feeling-thought-opinion, it's like holding our breath. We put the flow of experience on pause and obstruct the natural giving and receiving of life.

How did you feel in the role of *breather*? How did you feel being *breathed*? If you are doing this activity in a group, share your perceptions. I've used this exercise, created by Jim Ballard for William Pfeiffer and the University Associates' Series in Human Resource Development, numerous times with large groups. The participants have always been evenly divided. Some were most comfortable being in control; others found comfort in surrendering. Neither was right or wrong, merely more comfortable.

The ebb and flow of breathing presents a mighty metaphor. Nature's balance is patterned with opposites—winter releases into spring, night dawns day, blossoms fade away. When we accept the natural flow, we appreciate greater possibility. Light and dark become equally valuable. Appreciating both the giving and receiving of life, our growth doubles. Similarly to how you were able to quickly shift your approach to breathing with conscious attention, you can multiply your internal possibilities by being willing to remain flexible.

If you are a doer who likes to control, consider practicing surrender. Surrendering doesn't mean you accept the problem or its negative effects; you let go and release responsibility so other possibilities can be born.

If yours is a surrendering style, try embracing pro-activity. Consciously work to solve or resolve a situation. This shift can be invigorating. By learning how to be proactive, you increase your options.

What style of breathing is most comfortable for you—doing or surrendering? Where in your life is this style working? Not working? What might it look like if you shift to the opposite? Whenever you remain flexible enough to use your least comfortable style, you double your personal resources.

NON-GRASPING

Breathing teaches us that on the heels of every constriction is a fresh inspiration. Emptying, you are always refilled with the infinite supply of new life. Breathing is a constant reminder that receiving and releasing are natural. The present moment enters, you taste it, and gently let it go. Whatever the emotion or thought, you stay in the flow by savoring and releasing.

Meditation is a wonderful way to learn how to flow naturally with life. Creating a silent space, your mind can quiet all its busy activities of planning, sorting and assessing. Mind chatter that judges, critiques and criticizes is not the voice of the heart. Distracting noise enveloped in attitudes of **should**, reprimand or emotional reactivity are not to be confused with *inner truth*. Rather, these voices of childhood can be *thanked for sharing*, then allowed to float down the river of your thoughts.

The true voice of the heart is contained in silence. Here is where you connect with your deeper wisdom. Avoiding any stickiness, you can be a silent witness to your human feelings without attaching to them. Continually noticing, like counting sheep, you remain open to the next moment or thought without becoming entangled in the last one.

Similar to conscious breathing, you can intentionally welcome your thoughts and feelings, acknowledging them as bubbles effervescing throughout your experience. When you see the impermanence of its content, the vastness of the empty mind can be felt. Author Stephen Levine, defines this ". . . experience of this spaciousness [a]s the essence of non-grasping, of letting go, of having room for everything and holding to nothing. . . if fear or wanting arises, it is seen within the spaciousness that surrounds it. We don't get lost by becoming it, but simply see it as just another moment in the mind flow, another something which arose uninvited and will pass away in the same manner."

Now prepare for a journey. You will spiral down your breath into your heart and meet invisible, powerful forces that defy description. You may wish to read the meditation before you listen to the CD version.

Meditation

Into the Heart of the Matter

Prepare yourself for a wonderful journey into your heart of hearts. The following imagery will guide you into your soft center where you can access the wisdom of your nature. Find a quiet place where you won't be disturbed. Sit or lie in a position that is comfortable and supports a free flow of energy through your body. When you are ready, invite your eyes to close and the journey will begin.

Take a deep cleansing breath, exhaling through your mouth.
Focus on your breathing. Notice the air flowing in and out.
Inhale so that your breath fills your belly and travels all the way
down to your toes. With each exhale, breathe out all tension or
anxiety.
Imagine yourself swinging on each breath. Gliding forward
on each inhale, gracefully swing backward with each release.
Swing on your breath for a few minutes and enjoy the ride.
When you're ready, notice the precise point at which your
breath starts to come in and starts to go out. Without
changing anything except your attention, act as if the air is
breathing you. Let the air be the doer and reach down into you
and draw itself out.
Now reverse your point of view and act as if you are the doer.
Observe yourself as the one doing the breathing.

Now shift back again and act as if the air is breathing you. **Is there any change in your feelings when you surrender control?**

Which role is most comfortable?

How does this preference show up in your life?

Let these images and feelings fade.

Ride your breath deeply down into your soft center. Spiral farther down into your heart. . . Without critique or analysis, sense your heart, the container of your feelings. . . Notice what you see, sense and feel.

Look around and find the key to your heart. . . **Where is it kept? What does it look like?**

Delicately and with great love, find the entrance and use the key to open it.

Look around. **What do you sense? . . . What feelings flood your senses as your heart opens?** . . . Take a minute.

Here at the entrance stands the keeper of your heart who steps forward to greet you. **What does this being look like?** Ask what name it prefers. Without critique, let the name enter your mind.

Ask the keeper if it is willing to speak with you. If you get agreement, ask any questions you wish. Use whatever time you need to dialogue. Feel free to pause the CD.

When you are ready, look around your heart and find where you carry pain . . . **What does it look like? What color is it?**

Gently move your awareness into the center of this pain. . .

What do you experience? . . . To what relationships, situations or issues is the pain related? . . . Ask your heart if it would be willing to release this pain.

The keeper reveals to you the costs you are paying by
continuing to hold this pain and the rewards you could
reap by releasing it. Take a minute.
Ask the keeper of your heart if it would be willing to
release the pain by expressing it in journal writing following
this meditation. Let your mind bring up an image of the
best method for you to clear this pain.
When you are ready, look around and find where you carry
love. **What does it look like? What color is it? . . .**
Move your awareness into the center of this love. . . **To what
relationships, situations or issues is the love related?** Ask your
unconscious if it would be willing to continuously remind you
of these images of love. . . Let these images move to the perfect
site of accessibility, whether inside or around your body.
When you are ready, consciously inhale the color of love and
exhale the color of pain. Breathe in love and exhale pain . . .
until all that remains is love.

> **Ask the keeper of your heart if it automatically will activate
> this process whenever pain is present so your heart
> constantly generates its own healing. . .**
>
> Standing before you, the keeper of your heart invites you to
> remain in communication. Ask it how it can get your
> attention when repressed feelings are seeking recognition.
As you prepare to leave, decide if you wish to lock your heart
or leave it open. . . Determine where you wish to keep the
key. . . When you are ready, thank your heart and its keeper
for their generous sharing and tireless performance to sustain
your life.
Now, turn your awareness to the rest of your body.

What are you experiencing? . . .
Is there any tension, heaviness or tingling? Notice where, and let your attention move to one of these locations. Swim around in it and become aware of the sensations, feelings and thoughts stored here.
Allow the heaviness or tension to bubble up and rise at a safe pace toward your throat. Slowly watch the bubbles transform into words, feelings or thoughts. . . Take whatever time you need.
When you are ready, let the emotions and thoughts float up through you outwardly.
Relax and notice. You need not do anything with the thoughts or feelings. Merely acknowledge them in whatever way feels right to you. It is safe to express yourself. If tears are present, let them flow freely.
When you are ready, let yourself relax back into your body. Notice what it feels like. . . **Do you sense any differences in those parts of your body where you previously held tension or anxiety?**
What have you re-learned about yourself that you already knew? What have you learned about yourself that is new?
Invite an image of this newfound wisdom into your mind. . .
Ask it **"How can I incorporate you into my life?"** Take a minute to decide when you will be willing to affect this change.
Thank this image of new knowledge and ask it to move either inside or around your body to a location where you can be reminded of its content.

When you are ready, begin your journey back to the room.
Sense the walls around you and the surface beneath you.
Let your hands and feet return to their normal weight. When
you are ready, return fully by opening your eyes. Enjoy the
music, open to the journal writing exercise on the next page
and continue.

Journal Exercise

Into the Heart of the Matter

Describe the image of heart that came to you. What meaning did this vision hold? How can this image serve you?

Describe the keeper of your heart. What meaning does the keeper convey?

What color was the pain? What color was the love? Journal about each and the interconnection with certain relationships, issues and events in your life.

What did you feel like when you breathed in love and exhaled pain? How can you remind yourself consciously of this option?

What feelings were present in your body? What words, thoughts and feelings arose out of your sensations?

What was the most poignant image you saw and what did this image teach you?

Listening now to your inner voice, list any images or issues with which you need to continue working. When will you be willing to pursue this work?

How do you feel this moment? Please write freely any additional insights and experiences.

Go to www.innermagician.com to download journal pages for personal use.

75

Soulful Moment

Activity Suggestion

At least once during your initiation with the air element, rise early to see the sunrise. Notice at what point in the morning the birds begin to sing and listen to the variety of their songs. Breathe in the sun's fresh rays and imagine crystals of light filling every inch of your body like a battery storing vitality. Invite your body to use your breath to feel totally alive. Pay attention to your physical and emotional feelings, observing what sensations awaken.

or

Record a spontaneous soulful moment.

My Soulful Moment was _____ when I felt:

Metaphoric Insight

Activity Suggestion

Locate a nearby playground. Hop on a swing and play freely. Acting as a non-judgmental observer, pay attention to how you engage in these activities. Record your insight below.

or

Record a spontaneous Metaphoric Insight.

My Metaphoric Insight was _____ *when I felt:*

(To find possible metaphors, ask: How was your initial reaction to this assignment a metaphor for how you approach life? What did your method of locating a playground teach you about how you approach a task? How did your style of swinging offer a metaphor for some aspect of your life?)

Record the Wisdom Gleaned from Your Initiation with Air

Use both words and images freely as your imagination directs.

Ways I can incorporate this knowing into my life:

1.

2.

3.

Thank you Spirit for the life that fills me with each inhale
and the release I receive with each exhale.
Trusting that your abundance enters
me on the wings of breath,
I am always rich.

———

An Initiation with Water

Looking upon the river that runs through my soul,
I see clarity, rhythm and power.
Following my natural flow,
I embrace the many tributaries in unknown parts
of my heart and trace these waters
back to my origin.

A primary characteristic of water is fluidity. Ice, rain, snow, tears, floods, tidal waves, drink—the many forms of water reveal the diverse powers contained in its yielding gentleness. Within the element of water paradoxically lives life-giving and life-taking potential. Similarly, when we learn to be fluid, like water, we gain a wide range of possibilities; we also hold creative and destructive forces. Within water lies a profound metaphor. We can be:

Gentle like summer rain   CHILLING LIKE SNOW

Nurturing like a water fountain   **Destructive like flood**

Playful like bubbling stream   **SOLID LIKE ICE**

Powerful like avalanche   *Warm like hot springs*

By honoring our fluidity, we can flow effortlessly with the natural order, and we can harness both our creative and destructive powers. When we ignore this potential, we leave ourselves vulnerable to the influence of the unconscious power that lies frozen within.

This morning as I jogged by our neighborhood pond, partially frozen by the earlier night's chill, I spied an interesting scene. A band of geese were gathered for breakfast social hour—a feathered coffee klatch atop the hard, cold surface. Smiling, I thought, "What a great scene, geese walking on water." The image sent my mind tripping. Often we aspire, like the geese, to *walk on water*, hoping to transcend our humanness and remain above what we consider ugly. However, we pay a high price to remain atop the surface—our depth. Afraid of sinking into an abyss of unsightly emotions, we freeze our feelings . . . to remain above it all.

Sinking into our depths reminds us of our fallibility and can bring us to our knees; the child within experiences tears, anger and, ultimately, unworthiness. Our divinely endowed spirit is, however, the forgiving parent who loves unconditionally and revives our innate joy. In this moment of reunion between spirit and body, we have an epiphany.

This session is about trusting your natural ability to float in the sea of your being. Without fear of drowning, you can thaw the frozen emotions that have stolen your liveliness and spontaneity. You can claim your wholeness and honor your range of possibility.

A friend's recent experience taught me about how we abandon aspects of ourselves and leave them to roam homeless. Being inducted into a local church, he was dressed up in his three-piece suit, ready to receive his spiritual recognition. His pleasure faded swiftly, however, when a homeless person wandered into the church and sat immediately behind him as if his shadow. Extremely uncomfortable, my friend wished fervently that this vagrant would move away, but, like a magnet, the ragged wanderer hung close throughout the service.

Looking with metaphoric lenses on this scene, we see an important insight that gleams for all of us. At the moment in which my friend was calling forth his spiritual wholeness, a homeless person betrayed the truth. The vagrant who haunted my friend's induction metaphorically represented the aspects of himself that he had abandoned.

This bright, successful attorney had come to think of his mind and intellect as "who he was", but he is really much greater than these. Limiting himself in this way curtailed his true spirit and left him chronically depressed. His disowned parts manifested in the shape of the homeless shadow. My friend's expansive inner spirit waited, like his vagrant double, for the acknowledgment that would renew his wholeness.

Barbara DeAngelis, in her book, *Passion*, points out that the more logical we become, the more likely we let our mind talk us out of our feelings and we risk ending up being dry, hard and unreachable. When we closet those aspects of ourselves of which we are unaware, afraid or ashamed, we forfeit our inherent wholeness. The greatest tragedy is that we end up feeling as if we are frauds. Yet we fear that no one will love us if we invite our authentic Self home. Ironically, this thinking traps us into believing we are unlovable.

Like the 20,000-year-old woolly mammoth recently discovered beneath the Siberian ice, we too can recover parts of ourselves that have been in the deep freeze so long, they've become extinct. Bringing home these frozen orphans to a warm hearth and open vulnerability brings us to self-love. Claiming our wholeness means we integrate all of who we are, including our dark and golden shadows.

The Waters-of-Forgiveness meditation and writing exercise at the end of this chapter will help you defrost your *lost, buried* and *hidden* parts—orphans who wander homeless.

The *lost Self*, like the homeless man, is an aspect of which we were shamed during childhood. We learned to repress this aspect of Self so well that our conscious mind actually became unaware of its existence, except in the neurotic behaviors that flag its presence.

Rosita, a lovely woman of fifty-something, was delighted to discover her *lost Self* during a recent workshop. When asked to call forth an orphaned part of herself through her mind's eye, she saw a strong, charming Mexican man; intuitively she knew he symbolized her assertive strength. When asked where this aspect of herself had been hiding in her body, she felt a sudden pain in her hip and heard in her mind that she had been "sitting on him."

She had looked to the men in her life, especially her husband, to enact her active male energy. In fact, her husband had been heading up the business they operated mutually.

After integrating her disowned male side during this session's meditation, Rosita felt much stronger. She now knew she was sturdy enough to face the recent career challenge that had prompted her attendance in the workshop. In follow-up conversations, she reports that her husband is working in a new job as planned, and she is successfully running the business alone and loving it.

Similarly, when John engaged in the Waters-of-Forgiveness meditation, he was confronted with his feminine side, an aspect of himself he had deserted in the stern presence of his unemotional father. John's imagery came in the form of a homeless man pushing a shopping cart while dressed only in underwear.

When I asked John what he carried in the cart, his immediate image was "dolls." At six-foot-three and two-hundred-fifty pounds, John was very surprised by this spontaneous image! With some thoughtfulness, however, he acknowledged his gentle, caring nature and saw the important role it plays in his relationships. In the image of the cart filled with dolls, he saw the reflection of the big teddy bear of a man that others see in him.

The *buried Self* is usually an aspect of our personality we believe is bad; we believe that if we freely express it, we will be rendered unlovable. As a result, we frequently project onto those around us such feelings as anger and jealousy, and the desire to dominate.

Jeanette, a successful psychiatrist, uncovered this dynamic in herself as she experienced this meditation. When she invited her unconscious to bring forth an image of her *buried Self*, much to her surprise she looked on the face of her husband. His presence mirrored her need for control, an aspect of herself she had repressed due to a fear of rejection. In accusing him of being controlling, she had disowned her own need for control and let him act it out for both of them. Feeling dominated by her husband, she denied her desire to have things her way.

Jeanette had felt out of control because her power was invisible. Once she acknowledged her own wish to control, Jeanette gained a sense of being in charge of her life. Given his new balance of power, her husband was freed from being the villain, and conflict drained from their relationship.

The *hidden Self* represents the golden shadow, a positive aspect of Self that has been disowned due to some personal fear. My *hidden Self* showed up one morning as I lay half awake soon after I had written the Waters-of-Forgiveness meditation. A dream-like image of an old woman looking shriveled, dried up and bedridden, presented itself. Puzzled, my inquisitive mind asked, "Who is this person?" Quietly the answer drifted in, "Before you lies your Grandmother Wisdom. She lies dying because you have dismissed her. Thinking your age renders you too young to access the wisdom of the ages, you ignore her and she fades away."

Enlightened by this vision, I've had the opportunity to nurture a very rich aspect of myself which had shrunk into my unconscious. Periodically, I've rechecked this image in my mind to see how my Grandmother Wisdom is faring. Currently, her essence is very vibrant.

If an image appears that is hazy or vague, it signals an aspect of you that is not yet recognizable. If you are patient and attentive, the identity will eventually become clear. Laurie's vision brought up such a faceless figure in her mind during the Waters-of-Forgiveness meditation. Patiently, she waited for the figure's identity to be revealed, and it eventually showed up in a later meditation. This time, the figure's face was distinct, a wise "medicine woman," the part of Laurie she was now ready to claim.

FORGIVENESS

There is no pain or wound that cannot be healed. Beneath all human suffering lives our inherent divine wholeness. We are never broken. We cry, we suffer, we ache, we toil, but we are never broken.

Wholeness waits patiently beyond the door of forgiveness. We may journey long and hard or short and simple; we may remember our wholeness now or at our death. Regardless, the wellspring is never dry, and we can drink from the magic of our soul at any moment.

Like Dorothy in the Wizard of Oz, home is only as far away as the time it takes for us to click our heels together three times and say with conviction, "There's no place like home." In each minute, we can bring home our disowned Selves. It is never too late to forgive and remember.

Forgiveness is a conscious decision to embrace compassionately the human aspects of which we are ashamed. Continuing to push away what we don't like or fear about ourselves feeds on our energy and robs us of vitality. When we face that which we have orphaned, we gain a balanced heart. When we have nothing to hide, we are *free*. No matter how intense our pain, the potency of forgiveness is greater.

Gifted Native American healer Jamie Sams said, "Every time anyone seeks the silence of a balanced heart, the intuitive process can allow truth to come forward . . . When truth is found inside the Self, there is no need to look further."

The following meditation will bring home your orphans. Just as the physical body continuously gets dirty as a byproduct of ordinary life, the psyche also needs regular bathing. This session is one I hope you will revisit again and again.

Meditation

Bathing in the Waters of Forgiveness

Relax into a comfortable position and take a deep breath; settle
into yourself. Take another cleansing breath and exhale through
your mouth, reaching all the way down to your toes. Coming to
that place of total emptiness, hold your breath for just a
moment, then gradually begin a full inspiration. Feel the air
bathe every cell in your body with oxygen. Richly supplied,
your organs, muscles, bones and nerves shift into perfect
alignment. Your mind settles down just like a pebble gently
settles to rest on the bottom of a clear stream.
Immersed in this perfect nourishment, bring into your mind's
eye the image of an ocean beach. Feel the warm, fine sand
crunch under your feet. Smell the fresh salt air as the breeze
gently caresses your face. Hear the waves flowing out to the
horizon. Immerse yourself in the beauty, abundance and
serenity of your surroundings. Take a few minutes to smell,
see, touch and feel this special place.
As you sit in this place of natural beauty, you notice three
homeless orphans walking in the distance. As they approach,
you see that they represent the parts of yourself you have
disowned. Wandering aimlessly, they seek home.

**What do these figures look like? What are they
wearing?**
Notice what you feel as you behold them.
One of the castaways wishes to speak with you. S/he is
very adamant about gaining your attention and asks you to
hold counsel with her/him. Sit and face this figure. Notice
what this being looks like, how old s/he is.
**Ask this orphan why s/he wishes to go first? What disowned
part or parts of yourself does s/he represent?
What does this figure want? What blocked him/her from
getting this? What does s/he need from you in order to find a
safe harbor? Where in your body was this orphan hiding?
Listen to this wounded aspect of yourself.
As you pay attention to this being, does his/her appearance
change? If so, in what way?**
Communicate forgiveness to this abandoned part of yourself.
When you are ready, invite this aspect inside.
Slowly, the figure grows transparent and melds into you.
Take some time to notice how you feel. **How did your
body shift?**
The empty space now in front of you fills with a second
figure. Ask this being what disowned part of you s/he
represents? **Why did you abandon him/her? What is the
shame connected with him/her?** Dialogue until you both feel
understood. **Where in your body did this orphan live?**
When you are ready, embrace this outcast with forgiveness.
Once again, this form dissolves into you. Notice how you feel.
Now facing you is the last figure. Notice his/her appearance.
How is s/he dressed and what is his/her age?

Ask him/her what this castaway represents and why
s/he was cast out by you. Why did s/he wait until last?
What kept you from embracing this aspect of yourself?
What is it about yourself that feels so uncomfortable to
acknowledge that you hid it?
Quietly and gently move your awareness into the center of
the shape that sits before you. What do you learn as you
look out of these eyes?
When you are ready, return your awareness and look over at
the figure. Does s/he look any different? How?
Ask this figure where in your body s/he was hiding?
When you are ready, show forgiveness and compassion. How
does this person's appearance change?
Once again this displaced Self merges into you and you are
one. How does your body feel now?
As you look around this beautiful ocean scene, notice the
clearness of your vision.
Gazing about, glimpse a trail that you did not notice before.
The trail is lush with fresh green foliage and brilliant colored
blooms, and it disappears inland. As you walk the trail, you
feel centered and strong. The scents of the surrounding forest
fill your nostrils with sweetness.
Looking ahead, you spy several pools of spring water. Each
pool is encircled with rock outcroppings, and a small gentle
waterfall flows from one pool to the next. The waters
shimmer with a radiant glow; inner stillness has left the surface
looking like a sheet of liquid silver. Approaching the pools,
you sense a sacred aura.
These are the baths of forgiveness—birthing pools in the days

of the indigenous native. Today they birth your
wholeness.

Sit beside the pool of your choice and gaze into the
reflection of your soul.

When you know in your heart you are ready to truly
forgive yourself, wade into the sparkling water. As you
touch the pool's surface, an intense light appears in your
heart. It spreads throughout your body, then out into the
forest. You feel a divine flow of cleansing energy moving
through you. As you step fully into the waters, warm
soothing bubbles effervesce around you and flush away all
tension, guilt, anger and shame.

Immersed in these healing waters, you sink to the bottom.
Birthing your wholeness, you push off with supernatural
strength, spring up through the pool's surface and let out a
yell of freedom. Playing and splashing with light-heartedness,
you remember your original lightness. Play to your heart's
content.

When you are ready, float in perfect suspension, letting the
sun warm your body and the water gently lap against your
skin. A blue light enfolds your heart. Feel your openness
and invite images of the spiritual figures of your childhood;
they have special messages of forgiveness for you.
Take some time to bask, cleanse and heal in these divine waters.

Ever so gently, become aware of your surroundings. Feel your
fingers and toes, and let your limbs return to their normal
weight. When you are ready, open your eyes and begin the
journal writing exercise on the next page.

Journal Exercise

Bathing in the Waters of Forgiveness

What displaced parts of you did the three homeless orphans represent?

What meaning did you derive from your conversations with these figures?

Where were they hiding in your body? How do these locations correlate with any physical symptoms?

How does your body feel, now, in comparison with how you felt before the meditation?

What did you experience in the pools of forgiveness?

How often do you need to visit forgiveness? What will it take for you to be committed to this practice?

Please journal freely any additional insights or experiences.

Go to www.innermagician.com to download journal pages for personal use.

Soulful Moment

Activity Suggestion

Take a walk near a body of water and notice your experience. Watch how light and wind affect the surface of the water. Watch for swimming fish, animals and birds. Meditate on the interplay between sky, water and land. Record your experience below.

or
Record a spontaneous soulful moment.

My Soulful Moment was _____ when I felt:

Metaphoric Insight

Activity Suggestion

Find or create a pool or puddle of water. Play freely either with your whole body or hands and/or feet. Notice the movement of the water and how it feels. Uncover a personal metaphor. Record your experience below.

or

Record a spontaneous Metaphoric Insight.

My Metaphoric Insight was _____ when I felt:

Record the Wisdom Gleaned from Your Initiation with WATER

Use both words and images freely as your imagination directs.

Ways I can incorporate this knowing into my life:

1.

2.

3.

Stepping into my own stillness, I embrace all that I am.
Choosing to forgive my humanity,
I receive my divine inheritance.

———

An Initiation with Fire

Flame of my passion burn brightly and mirror my heart's desire.
Feed my soul with love and warm my heart with vision.

First seen in the natural forms of lightning bolts, searing lava and glaring sunlight, fire was discovered to be essential for the survival of our ancestors, and therefore, sacred. Regarded as a true gift of the gods, a public holy fire burned at all times. Such a special flame has been alive for more than 3,000 years in a holy temple near the Ganges River in India.

In our body's sacred center we, too, have a holy fire that burns continually. This is the flame of life that constantly pulses life energy throughout our body. The visceral experience of life that flows from this fire is felt as passion. The flare of passion dances within, and we feel the exquisite sensation of being vigorously alive.

Conceived in passion, we have a hunger for the "complete emotional absorption, that magical moment when we are swept away, finally free from everyday rules, restraints, and routines . . . Passion is what happens when we let go of control . . . [when we are] in love with life," describes Barbara de Angelis in her book, *Passion*.

When we embrace our passion, it's like riding a thunderbolt through the universe. With heightened awareness, our vision seems very clear, colors more vibrant, beauty magnified. We see significance and magnificence all around. The world seems a place filled with wonder, and we revel in understanding its mysteries. Passion is the true essence of life.

We love the expansiveness, the unbridled energy and the euphoria of passion. On the other hand, our human nature fears facing the unknown, taking risks and making changes. We sometimes use indifference to numb this natural desire. Overwhelmed with fears of being hurt, embarrassed or out of control, we may choose the known rather than the mysterious.

No wonder we love to throw ourselves into the passion of professional sports. Sitting safely in our favorite armchair, we can feel intense anticipation, excitement and euphoria without taking personal risks, making any changes or losing control. However, there is a big difference between making love and watching others engage in lovemaking.

When we open to our natural passion, there is no room for fear or feeling unworthy. There is only truth, the truth of our being. We immerse ourselves into each moment of life, trusting our sense of Self, the integrity of our heart.

This session's meditation invites you to move into your passionate center and begin leading with your heart. By courageously embracing your raw feelings, you can taste the color and texture of passion. The reward is vibrant energy.

In the same way that electricity releases energy to produce heat, light and a multitude of domestic conveniences, passion fuels our creative energy and anchors us in the moment. Joan Borysenko, respected scientist and author, has affirmed that as long as we are passionate about our dreams, we have the energy to bring them into manifestation. This belief was echoed recently by a Dutch psychologist who tried to determine what separated chess masters and chess grand masters. Subjecting groups of each to a battery of tests—IQ, memory, spatial reasoning—he found no testing differences. The discerning factor was that the grand masters simply loved chess more; they had more passion and commitment to it. Passion ignited the creative energy that spawned grand masters.

BOLD AND BOUNDARIED

I challenge you to be *bold* and *boundaried*, loving each moment of life passionately while being aware of your own and others' boundaries. Like a campfire that burns freely within its rock circle, you can feel intensely without harming yourself or others.

When we cross over our boundaries and burn out of control, we leave behind our sacred center. The inner flame of our heart is abandoned while our craving for excitement engulfs all around us. Forest fires are not caused by fire alone; they are created in the absence of boundaries. When passions are allowed to burn out of control, they cause damage with impulsive and indiscreet behavior. Boundaries, however, establish the safety for us to experience our passion fully. Remember: bold and boundaried!

When was the last time you felt truly passionate about something? What dreams have you committed to? What fuels your passion?

The following meditation connects you with your passion. You'll have the opportunity to build your sacred fire, establish your boundaries and witness your soul's flame. Light a candle to burn before you during the meditation and the journal writing exercise that follows.

Meditation

Tending the Inner Fire, Seat of Your Passion

Close your eyes and let your body ease into a natural position.
Smooth and relax your muscles as you settle into a perfect resting
position. Breathing deeply, allow air to fill your lungs, then carry
nutrients to replenish every cell in your body.

Imagine a bright light entering the crown of your head and
slowly moving through your entire physical Self. Waves of
relaxation penetrate the back of your head, your face and your
neck; they flow down through your chest and abdomen, then
spread into your arms and hands. The light moves on
through your pelvis, your legs and your ankles until it gently
exits through the bottoms of your feet.

Now gently move your awareness inward, to that space of
inner wisdom, where you will learn to tend your inner fire—the
seat of your passion.

There, in your mind's eye, ask your unconscious mind to bring
up an image of a place in nature, a beautiful spot that is safe and
powerful.

What are the contours and colors of this natural sanctuary?

Notice the smells and sounds. Feel the temperature of
the air against your skin.
Looking to the horizon, the lavender skyline tells you it is
dusk and you see or sense the sun sinking in the west.
Notice the colors and cloud formations. **What feelings or
sensations do you have?**
Deciding to make a fire to bring warmth and light, you gather
fallen branches and twigs and arrange them in a pile beside
you. Look around for rocks to encircle the flames. As you
arrange them in preparation for your campfire, notice the color,
size and texture of each rock. They are the guardians of your
sacred fire, the seat of your inner passion.
After you have arranged the rocks, build a fire with the wood
you have collected and light it. Matches lay on the ground
beside you.
**What happened as you tried to ignite the flame? Did the fire
start easily? If not, what made it difficult?**
Tend your fire until it develops steady flames. Hold it with
your gaze and feed it as needed.
Observe the frequency with which the flames must be fed in
order to maintain a constant supply of warmth and light.
Sitting beneath a starry sky, watch the flashes of orange, red
and blue dance before you. Hear the crackling of the wood,
feel the warmth and sense the radiant glow of your sacred fire.
Staring intently into the flames, you see a vision. This is an
image of you when your inner fire is dim or going out. Notice
your appearance and behavior.
How does this state of mind feel?
Ask this image what led to this lack of fire. What caused this

absence of passion? What are the events, feelings or
issues that drown out the flame in your soul? Listen
carefully.
Whatever feelings bubble up, let them be expressed. There
is no need to withhold.
Whenever you are ready, thank this image and let it fade
back into the campfire.
Holding a steady gaze, ask the flame for yet another image.
This time, bring up a picture of you when your inner fire
burns out of control and escapes its boundary burning outside
the circle of rocks. What does your life look like at these times?
How do you feel? What are the consequences?
Thanking the flames, let this image fade back into the tended fire
encircled by the earthen rocks.
Next, ask the fire to conjure up images of the kinds of fuels
necessary for your unique inner passion? Where and how can
you acquire these? What must you do to consistently feed
your inner flame?
Thank these images and let them fade.
There is someone with whom you need to speak in order
to nourish your inner flame. This person stands in the
shadows waiting. If you are willing, invite him/her to join you
at the campfire. Sit face-to-face and speak your peace as this
person listens. Dialogue until there is clarity between you.
Take some time.
Thank this person for the visit and watch him/her walk away
into the darkness.
Ask the flames for one final image. This is a vision of you
when your inner flame is ignited and your passion connects

you with your heart. **What do you look like?**
What personal characteristics do you display?
Look into these eyes and witness your natural vibrancy.
Gently and steadily move your awareness into the center of
this passionate, enlivened being and look out at the world.
How do you feel?
Looking from this perspective, see the people with whom you
are in love. Witness the dreams and experiences that nourish
passion and commitment within you.
Feeling the constant warmth of the inner flame that burns in
your heart, notice how you feel sitting before this roaring
campfire. Grounded with the earth and fueled with the natural
life force, it protects you from the cold and lights your darkness.
Thank it for its stories that have given you new sight.
Looking back over the night's events, notice what you learned
about yourself. **What did you learn that is new?**
What did you relearn?

When you are ready, let these thoughts and images gradually
fade as you journey back into this room.
Become aware of the surface that supports you. As your arms
and legs return to normal weight, you regain feeling in your
fingers and toes.
When you are ready, open your eyes and begin the journal
writing exercise on the next page.

Journal Exercise

Tending the Inner Fire, Seat of Your Passion

What feelings, events and issues cause your passion to dim?

With whom do you need to hold council in order to keep your sacred fire burning consistently? What is it you need to help them understand?

What experiences, feelings or relationships fuel the light of your soul?

How can you ignite your passion?

What did you learn about maintaining an appropriate boundary for your inner passion?

When are you most likely to cross boundaries? How do you know when you cross a boundary?

Please journal freely any additional insights or experiences.

Go to www.innermagician.com to download journal pages for personal use.

111

Soulful Moment

Activity Suggestion

Remember back to a time when you felt passionate and alive. What did you feel in your body? What did you feel emotionally? How did you behave? What was the source of this passion? Record your responses below.

or

Record a spontaneous Soulful Moment.

My Soulful Moment was _____ when I felt:

Metaphoric Insight

Activity Suggestion

Light a campfire or several candles. Watch the dancing flames and look for patterns and images. What metaphor is revealed? Record your experience below.

or

Record a spontaneous Metaphoric Insight.

My Metaphoric Insight was _____ when I felt:

Record the Lessons Gleaned from Your Initiation with FIRE

Use both words and images freely as your imagination directs.

Ways I can incorporate this knowing into my life:

1.

2.

3.

Thank you, flame of my soul, for the love that surrounds me
and opens my eyes to the world's magnificence.

I am joy.

———

Synthesis

Spirit of my soul, you mirror a creative and loving Universe.
Shining in my eyes is the golden light of a million stars.
My consciousness reaches to the edge and
sees that I am connected with all.
I am that I am that I am.

The previous four initiations with the elements of *Earth, Air, Water* and *Fire* have illumined your vision, raised your inner voice and recorded your story. This process has transformed or renovated inner structures. Perhaps you remodeled a room or two or maybe you totally gutted the house and rebuild it.

The work of personal transformation is not to be taken lightly. It requires focused energy and time. You require integration time as you transition through these changes. Although the effort is not physically visible, it can be exhausting—as well as exhilarating. People around you may wonder at your level of absorption with something invisible. Yet the work of personal transformation is work of the soul. Ralph Waldo Emerson said, "No matter where we go or what we do, it is the work of the Self we are about."

The following session integrates the previous four initiations. In Volume Two, you will have the opportunity to go deeper; however, it is important, now, to take whatever time you require to integrate and to avoid being overwhelmed. If you've ever done a remodeling project, remember back to the degree your life was in disarray during the work. Similarly, inner projects take a chunk of time to determine one's authentic design, enact it and clean up before you can really enjoy the fruits of your labor.

ENCIRCLING THE LESSONS

The following exercise will help you bring the various lessons into a coherent whole. Take a minute to refer back to the final page in each session where you identified the primary lessons you wished to remember. Copy them onto the circle in each of the four directions: north, south, east and west. If any lessons seem related, or in opposition to each other, position them at opposite poles.

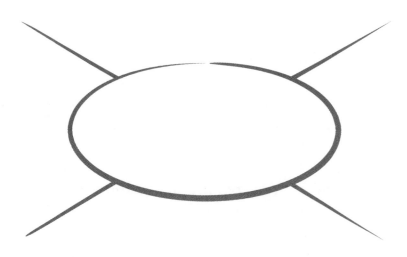

Write your previously collected insights around the circle and then read the following brief meditation.

Meditation

Synthesis

The following meditation will illuminate how the previous four lessons can be implemented within your life. Take a few minutes in a still posture.

Close your eyes and imagine a TV. This wizard's screen allows you to see a movie of your life. In your mind's eye, push the play button. Take a minute to watch.

Now, rewind the video and assume the role of Director. You have the magical ability to project your life video in such a way that you respect your newly learned lessons. Direct the actors in whatever way you wish. . .Take some time. . .

How does your life look with these lessons incorporated?
What new possibilities are revealed?. . . How do you feel in this new version? . . .

Breathing through your heart, notice the word that represents your inner feeling.

What image represents the simultaneous realization of these lessons? . . . Move this image inside or around your body to a location where it can help you integrate the changes.

Now open your eyes.

Draw a picture of this image and word. Give your imagination free rein to draw and decorate in whatever ways feel right to you.

Go back to the circle on page 118. In the center, jot the goals, dreams, behaviors, attitudes and feelings that integrate the four lessons. These items describe the range of possibility that lies in the territory where they overlap. Let's use Sally's lessons as an example.

Session one: My inner child needs more play time.

Session two: I want to be emotionally present with my family.

Session three: I reclaim that part of me that wants attention.

Session four: Focusing on pleasing others causes my passion to dim.

Look over the specific lessons in the above list. Then put the pieces of the puzzle together.

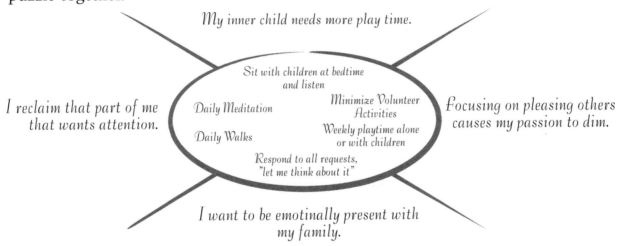

My inner child needs more play time.

I reclaim that part of me that wants attention.

Focusing on pleasing others causes my passion to dim.

Sit with children at bedtime and listen

Daily Meditation

Minimize Volunteer Activities

Daily Walks

Weekly playtime alone or with children

Respond to all requests, "let me think about it"

I want to be emotinally present with my family.

Notice the opposing struggle between taking care of oneself and focusing outward toward others. Energy is drained away by people-pleasing, while attention given to nurture the Self generates energy. Thus, people-pleasing steals energy that could be spent on Self and family.

To dismantle this need for others' approval, Sally must practice loving herself unconditionally. Paying consistent attention to her inner child will liberate her inner playmate who can engage with her children and spouse in wonderful ways. If Sally nurtures her soul daily and minimizes people-pleasing behavior, she can generate the energy to be emotionally present with her family. This may sound very simple; in fact, these issues can feel very difficult.

Now it is your turn. You have a personal truth. Only you will know how to fit together the pieces of your unique puzzle. Sally's puzzle is likely to be different from Jane's, although their core issues may be similar. There are no right or wrong answers, only personal truth that *FEELS AUTHENTIC*.

Look over your list of lessons and find the puzzle that fits together for you. Write down your insights so you can remember your truth whenever you notice old habits sneaking up on you.

CHANGE! DON'T CHANGE!

External support is critical to the process of structural change. Attempts to grow can be disconcerting to those around you, especially if it means you respond to them differently. Spouses, children and parents may not give you support for making the changes you desire. They are the main characters in your life story, and they may become afraid of being written out of your new script. In fact, if your changes cause a relationship to be edited, that person may actively resist.

Janet found this to be the case when she progressed through the *Inner Magician* sessions. As she gained clarity about herself, she realized she struggled with depression because she obsessively attempted to care-take and please others. Through her journey of self-discovery, she began to say "no" more often and to create solitary time for walking and meditating. As a result, Janet felt happier and more content. Although her husband greatly enjoyed having a lighter climate at home, he began to complain about his job and his unmet needs. He saw how Janet was evolving, and he was confused and jealous.

Janet was very tempted to abandon her changes because she felt guilty and unsure of herself. However, the thought of returning to her previous state of mind was untenable. Rather, she engaged her husband in the process of remodeling their relationship so it would accommodate both their needs. Many passionate conversations later, they have arrived at a new balance. Their mutual soul-searching resulted in a rearranging of his work to allow him more free time for personal and shared play time.

To save herself from abandoning her desired changes, Janet sought several sources of external support: an occasional session with a therapist, weekly attendance at a personal-growth class and regular contact with people she knew had gone through a similar journey. These support systems offered Janet the validation she needed, and she is very pleased with the way her life is growing.

Seek affirmation for the changes you are making! If you choose to take this journey with a group, this circle of people may be an excellent place to gather your support. In addition, arrange times to connect regularly with people who will advocate unleashing your authentic Self.

Take a minute now to visualize those souls whom you trust to support your desired change.

Close your eyes and sense those people you know will support your growth. They stand in a loving circle around you. Take some time to go around the circle and hear a supportive message from each; then, open your eyes and write their names and messages below:

Similarly, it is important to identify who is unable to provide you with support at this vulnerable time. These people usually are not intentionally trying to block your growth; they are concerned with their own safety and security needs. Understanding this, you can protect yourself from exposure until you are stronger and ready to hold your own. With some people, it may mean you choose to minimize shared time. With those people whom you must be in regular contact, you may decide to limit personal disclosures about your process. This decision has nothing to do with whether you love or care for someone. Rather, it is establishing boundaries that keep you safe so that you may engage in these relationships without compromising who you are. Many times when you share your dreams with others who are known to be critical, you hand over our personal power.

Take a few minutes to sense the people in your life with whom you must hold firm boundaries during this vulnerable time of transition.

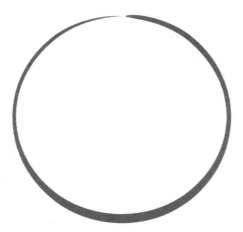

Gently close your eyes and go inward. In your mind's eye, draw a circle around yourself at whatever distance feels right. See the images of the people with whom you must keep clear boundaries during this time of change. They are standing outside your sacred circle. When you are ready, write down the names of these people.

Now is the time to fully claim your power, beauty and wisdom. Your channels are open to the creative forces of the universe, and you can use them to create the life you deserve. Like a plant that has been transplanted into a bigger pot so it can expand, you have broadened your horizons. Bask in the sun, fertilize your beautiful nature and watch yourself flourish.

Gather the insights, visions and memories you have collected during this four-session journey. Keep them as touchstones that can guide you *home* whenever you become lost. When you wonder or worry how to stay aligned with your inner truth, return to these meditations and journal entries to find your answers—they will point the way back to your heart.

Engaging in this life-changing work, the work of the soul, is not always easy, but it is the most important work of our lives. When we transform, the world transforms. To honor our authentic Selves without harming others is an accomplishment of huge magnitude.

When you are ready to continue your adventure, *Releasing the Inner Magician, Book Two, A Deepening* (released soon) awaits; it allows you to intensify your growth and incorporate transformation as a way of life. Elemental forces continue to provide the backdrop for powerful meditations.

The first initiation with earth takes you spelunking through the caves of your mind where you bring unconscious dark shadows of the Self to light and transform them.

The element of air in the second session teaches you about change as a natural progression. The journey from caterpillar to butterfly is offered as the perfect metaphor for guiding you to liberate yourself from old patterns and take flight into new possibilities.

An initiation with water in session three deeply cleanses past emotional debris and helps you envision future dreams.

The metaphor in session four is fire as you burn away old guilt and shame, and step into your inherent magnificence. In your imaginary magician's robes, you find five secret pockets that contain powerful wisdom about your life.

You are the hero of your personal story. Live well and enjoy!

Closing Meditation

We are part of a magic circle. Hands linked in the mystery of
life, our echoes resound so loudly that the world must respond.
I sense the glow of my soul, and I feel the radiance of other
souls standing with me. Slowly and gently, I let my inner light
dance through me and out into the room; I feel the infinite
energy drawn from the Source flow through me and out into
the world. This whirl of radiance hovers over all that is
parched with conflict and grief. Love penetrates like a sponge
drinking water. As my mind circles the world, earth's vibrant
colors and texture imprint my memory. Gently, my light
returns to the rich soil of my core where a seed germinates and
sprouts a blossom. I carry this bloom always; it is a reflection
of my inner beauty!

*"Magic is nothing but the wisdom of the Creator
revealed and planted in the creature."*
Thomas Vaughan, 17th century scholar/magician

———

ACKNOWLEDGMENTS

When I returned from my sabbatical in Australia, I had a vivid dream in which I was pregnant and about to give birth. I believe this dream was a personal revelation predicting this book's emergence from the womb of my experience. Now in the christening stage, I thank the many midwives in attendance.

Turaya master Laurie Seymour and Turaya founder Dawn Taylor awakened my awareness to universal energies. They taught me to trust the natural flow of wisdom that is always available, and I am deeply grateful for their wise guidance. Similarly, Dr. Roger Teal, Rev. Majorie Staum, Rev. Patty Luchenbach, Rev. Lloyd and Shekina Barrett of the Mile High Church of Religious Science have provided invaluable instruction and support in the journey of my own soul, and I thank them.

Professionally, I am grateful to Drs. Martin Rossman and David Bresler who taught me the art of Interactive Guided Imagery and to Drs. Stephen Gilligan and David Cheek who taught me Ericksonian Hypnosis techniques. These methods, in addition to Jung's Active Imagination and Somatic Therapy out of New Zealand, laid the groundwork for creating the intuitive meditations in this book. Similarly, I thank Imago master teacher Maya Kollman for an introduction to the concept of lost aspects of Self.

Steve Weist of International Sound Studios is a gifted musician and recording professional. He made the experience of recording these meditations one of magic. I came to rely upon his support and wonderfully positive energy. This CD is his creation and I am truly thankful.

Graphic artist Mark Gelotte intuitively perceived the essence of this book and deftly translated it into a compelling, mystical cover and chapters artistically arranged to flow like poetry. He was a joy to work with and always kept his calm presence even when my indecision caused him more work. I thank Mark for his gracious and talented partnering.

Dorothy Elder, Charol Messenger, Carol Montgomery, Barbara Blair, Kris Kelman, Barbara McNichol, and Christine Pacheco are all angels for their willingness to review and edit the manuscript. Their comments and personal support were invaluable. I can't thank them enough.

To the members of my writers group, Marjorie Tyler, Mimi Shannon, Barbara Blair, and Betsy Rubin, I send warmest regards. They created a comfortable nest to which I could return as I was learning to fly on my own. Each is a blessing.

I am grateful for Karen Dannewitz and Kay Lutts and their generous invitation to include me in creating personal growth workshops. Our mutual experiences offered invaluable lessons in the art of experiential learning and my own personal transformation.

Thank you to the friends and clients whose stories are included. I admire their courage and willingness to explore their soulfulness.

Having hit my mid-life stride, I realize the inner wealth I inherited. I blow a kiss of gratitude and love to my mother in Kansas and to my father beyond.

Finally, I acknowledge those whom I take for granted most often and whom sacrificed the most for the birth of this book—my family. I am deeply thankful for my soulful playmate of twenty-one years, Dick Fullerton. His willingness to challenge me out of my comfort zone keeps me eternally learning. Our children Walker and Elena enrich my life with laughter and tears, and are more dear to me than I would have thought possible.

I thank Spirit for these marvelous gifts and for the Divine inspiration that sprung up between the lines.

SOURCES

Baldwin, Christina. *Life's Companion, Journal Writing as a Spiritual Quest.* New York: Bantam Books, 1991, pg. 9.

Borysenko, Joan. *The Ways of the Mystic, Seven Paths to God.* California: Hay House, Inc. 1997.

Cameron, Julia. *The Artist's Way.* California: Jeremy P. Tarcher, 1992.

Chatwin, Bruce. *The Songlines.* London: Picador, 1988.

De Angelis, Barbara. *Passion.* New York: Delacorte Press, 1998.

Dossey, Larry, M.D. *Recovering the Soul.* New York: Bantam Books, 1989.

Emerson, Ralph Waldo. *Essays by Ralph Waldo Emerson with Introduction by Irwin Edman.* New York: Harper & Row Publishers, 1951, pg. 99, 190.

Havecker, Cyril. *Understanding Aboriginal Culture.* Australia: Cosmos Periodicals, 1987.

Gendlin, Eugene. *Focusing.* New York: Bantam Books, 1978.

Jahn, Robert and Dunne, Brenda. *Margins of Reality.* New York: Harcourt Brace Jovanovich, 1987.

Pfeiffer, J. William (editor). Ballard, Jim (source). *The 1989 Annual Developing Human Resources.* California: University Associates, 1989, pgs. 47-54.

Raff, Jeffrey. *Jung and the Alchemical Imagination.* York Beach, Maine: Nicholas-Hayes, Inc., 2000.

Saal, Rollene. *The New York Public Library Guide to Reading Groups.* New York: Crown Publisher, 1995.

Sams, Jamie and Carson, David. *Medicine Cards.* New Mexico: Bear and Company, 1988.

Sams, Jamie. *Sacred Path Cards.* New York: Harper Collins Publishers, 1990.

Von Oech, Roger. *A Whack On the Side of the Head.* New York: Warner Books, 1983.

Walsch, Neale Donald. *Conversations with God, Book 1.* Virginia: Hampden Roads, 1995.

Wood, Nancy (poetry) and Howell, Frank (paintings). *Dancing Moons.* New York: Bantam Doubleday Dell Publishing Group, 1995.

HOW TO CONTACT THE AUTHOR

Deborah Sandella offers workshops, retreats, and individual sessions for the purpose of personal growth, healing, and transformation. These offerings can be found at www.innermagician.com. Inquiries for speeches and seminars can be directed to her through the website or by calling 303-691-3457.